Punished For Working

Theresa Diiti

IngramSpark

One Ingram Blvd.
La Vergne, TN 37086
(615) 793-5000
www.ingramspark.com

Copyright © 2016 Theresa Diiti

Cover design by Daryl Gray

Visit us at www.theresadiiti.com
All rights reserved.

This book or any portion thereof may not be reproduced or used in any manner whatsoever without the express written permission of the publisher except for the use of brief quotations embodied in critical articles and book reviews.

Printed in the United States of America

First Printing, 2018
ISBN 9781849149341
ISBN 1849149348

IngramSpark is a service operated by Lightning Source to cater for the needs of independent publishers and authors. LaVergne, Tennessee USA

Because of the dynamic nature of the Internet, any web addresses or links contained in this book may have changed since publication and may no longer be valid. The publisher is not responsible for websites (or their content) that are not owned by the publisher. The information in this book is true and complete to the best of our knowledge. To protect the privacy of certain individuals the names and identifying details have been changed. The content of this book is the sole expression and opinion of its author, and not necessarily of the publisher. Neither the publisher nor the individual author shall be liable for any physical, psychological, emotional, financial, or commercial damages, including, but not limited to, special, incidental, consequential or other damages. You are responsible for your own choices, actions and results. The author and publisher disclaim any liability in connection with the use of this information. All recommendations are made without guarantee on the part of the author or IngramSpark

This book is presented solely for education and entertainment purposes .The author and publisher are not offering it as legal or other professional services advice.

Books may be ordered through booksellers, IngramSpark or by contacting www.theresadiiti.com

Mama, you let nothing stop you from going to work, you made me so proud! Because of you, I have a strong work ethic, and you will never have to worry about my ability to take care of myself. Being independent and self-sufficient is the most valuable gift that you could ever give me. Thank you; I love you.

*"You need money, and to have money,
you have to work and never let anything go by."*

(Edith Flagg)

What was the most lasting and meaningful thing ever said to me? "You're ahead of your time."

CONTENTS

Introduction—Who are my readers? xi

1 Exemptions 1

2 Disclaimer 3

3 The Meeting 5

4 Love at First Paycheck 13

5 Plates as Big as States 25

6 So Humbly Sad to Meet You 39

7 Hail that Ambulance! My Doctors Don't Cost a Thing 51

8 Not Working for the Children 63

9 One Way or Another 75

10 Solid as Smoke 83

11 Strategies – CEOs and Millionaires Could Learn a Thing or Two 89

12 Stamp 'Em Through, Get Paid, and Shut Up! 103

13 Previous answers from Theresa Diiti published on Quora 107

14 Acknowledgments 171

15 References 173

Notes 179

INTRODUCTION

Who are my readers?

Working people who, be it rain, sleet, snow, or hail, still have to go to work.

Working people who teach their children that "Yep, this is what it's like being a grown-up. You have to work, sometimes wherever the job is or however much it pays, in order to support yourself."

Working people who have to pay full price for everything, including food, and then watch their paychecks evaporate before their eyes.

Working people who are just plain sick and tired of being *Punished for Working*.

CHAPTER 1

Exemptions

Ok, before the hairs start standing up on the back of everyone's necks, please know that there are some *exemptions* to what is said in this book, by which I mean that there are certain people to whom my observations don't apply. This is not a "one-size-fits-all situation" by any means. For example, if you have worked all your life to raise a family and survive, you fall into the exempt category. If you've found yourself suddenly unemployed through no fault of your own, you, too, are exempt. If you have to get up before the roosters and, go to work whether it's raining, snowing, or worse, you're exempt!

If you have ever had to leave one job only to make it across town to work another job later the same day, exempt, exempt, exempt! But there's more: if you have to plan your meals for the next two weeks because the remaining twenty-dollar bill in your pocket will just *have* to last until next payday, exempt again! If you were raised to believe that it is your responsibility to raise your children and no one else's—you guessed it, and you're exempt.

Lastly, if you were raised to believe that you could rise above poverty but that it takes effort to do so, exempt, exempt, exempt again! I could go on all day, but by now you should have figured out whether this book is going to stimulate some conversations in your house—I bet it will.

CHAPTER 2

Disclaimer

If, by chance, you feel a slight elevation of your blood pressure, or your nostrils start flaring, or your eyebrows shoot up, don't be surprised: these are normal reactions for those who read *Punished for Working*. Some readers have reported feeling the need to go outside in the backyard and build something or tear something up. Some have found themselves turning the TV or radio down just to make sure that they understood what they just read. Others have felt need to grab a quick beer or glass of wine, or both. Don't worry, though; everyone ends up being okay.

Punished for Working is not a fairy tale, nor did I intend it to be. It started out as a journal in which I recorded some of the funny situations that I encountered during the workday, but, once I reflected on these situations, I realized that they weren't actually funny at all. Instead, I started noticing that the population that

I worked with was winning the argument hands-down, proving that the perks of *not* working can outweigh the benefits of being employed-especially when dependence on assistance programs goes on for generations.

So, in this disclaimer, I must add that the content of these pages is by no means meant to disparage anyone who has had the misfortune of losing a job. The book does, however, offer a frank look at individuals who have managed to devise every way imaginable to avoid working, depending instead on assistance programs, and doing so quite nicely. Could this be the reason that dependence on social service programs has grown at an exponential rate over the past few decades?

This book is based solely on my own very real and personal experiences and is in no way representative of *all* individuals, working or otherwise, who utilize public assistance programs.

CHAPTER 3

The Meeting

I met with a publisher at the beginning of this project and let him read a few pages of *Punished for Working*. I informed him that the manuscript had started as a diary of my humorous and shocking experiences as a social services professional. During our conversations about the book, he exclaimed, "You've got something here!" He explained that many people, including him, had no idea about how public assistance works or its impact on the lives of the people that receive it. He went on to say that he would like to learn more and was sure others would be interested as well. Thus, the project continued, though it has been laid to rest and resurrected more times than Freddy Krueger.

Some years have passed since our conversation but this book still seems relevant to the lives of average Americans. The world that I describe is pretty much the one that we are living in now—we are working, not working, doing what we have to do or what we have always been accustomed to doing. When I first started writing, it seemed that those of us who were working were being punished because, even though we had jobs, we were barely getting by and didn't qualify for any additional help to make it through to the next paycheck. Now, we're seeing that some of those who were employed before the pandemic are without a paycheck and in need, but they and their families are being left out in the cold.

When I would try to motivate myself to get back to the keyboard, I would sometimes wonder, *A hundred years from now, who's going to know about it anyhow?* Then something in the news would spark my interest, and I would feel the drive to finish telling my story. So, here are a few questions. First, if you have already received your wages for the month and you fail to return to the worksite to finish the duties that you were paid to perform, who's left holding the bag? Is it you, the worker who failed to show up, or is it the business owner? Of course, it's the business owner–but there's more. What if you, the undependable worker, continued to receive pay even though you chose not to report to work? Would this situation encourage you to start reporting to work or just to stay home because, either way, you're being compensated? If any of this made sense, I wouldn't have written *Punished for Working*.

I asked hundreds of people, okay, more like one hundred people these same questions, and most of them responded, "Nope, it doesn't make any sense at all!" But this happens every day in the life of a social service worker, especially when we are tasked with helping our clients find employment. It may not happen exactly the same way in every case, but it's pretty close. The current structure of assistance programs unintentionally, I'm sure, discourages people from working regardless of the approach that we take. While we encourage our clients to work instead of remaining on public assistance, we meet resistance because working appears less lucrative "perk-wise" and a whole lot harder. The fear of losing benefits as a result of getting a job, especially for those whose families have depended on social services programs for generations, is just too great. If being employed causes a loss of free benefits for a household, working could be viewed as counterproductive or even punishment.

In my opinion—and I do say "in my opinion" a lot—allowing people to depend on social service programs does more harm than good because dependence removes the desire or drive to get ahead by working. The resistance that I met when trying to "pump up" the idea of accepting the job placements that we offered just made for a long day. Please keep in mind that dependence on programs is the key issue here because some of our programs have become a way of life for families. Trying to persuade, entice, convince, sweet-talk, and even beg clients to trade the guaranteed first-of-the month payday that most public assistance programs provide for waking up to an alarm clock, getting dressed and being somewhere on time on a regular schedule well, for some, all of this is just too much to ask.

Don't get me wrong: assistance programs can be life-savers, especially for individuals who have found themselves recently unemployed because of unforeseen developments like the coronavirus pandemic. During the crisis that we're in now, programs that help recipients to secure or maintain housing, keep their utilities on, buy necessities, and, in many cases, feed their families, are more important than at any time I can remember in my life. Some assistance programs try to instill a sense of responsibility by setting requirements, but I found while working in the field that they are not very effective when it comes to ensuring that the recipients keep up their end of the bargain. Some states do reduce the amount of monthly assistance for those who fail to report to work sites, for example, but these measures have not proved effective, being met with responses such as "Go ahead and take it!" or "Do what you gotta do!"

By now, you may be asking, is this book about working, not working, or assistance programs? In fact, it is about all of the above. What prompted me to start paying close attention to the administration of these programs was my observation of patterns that I kept seeing in my clients and their families. As I said, some of my experiences were the stuff of comedy and others the stuff of horror, but, in every case, I kept coming back to the thought that we created this. I became concerned when I realized that some of our clients seemed to have the idea that the assistance programs on which they depended, sometimes for years–would never end.

Fifty or sixty years ago, applying for public assistance was the absolute last resort. However, at least for some of my clients who were long-term recipients of social services, relying on public assistance was the obvious preference over working. They seemed to have developed the mindset that they would continue to be taken care of in one way or another and were relatively unconcerned about the possibility that the assistance programs might be eliminated. It almost seems like working is no longer mandatory since individuals' basic needs are already being met through one assistance program or another. Generational recipients especially seem to think that their survival is essentially guaranteed through assistance programs without their having to work–so, they think, *why should I work*?

While conducting research in preparation for writing this book, I came across David Shipler's *The Working Poor*[1] and thought about how things were when it was published compared with how they are now. He wrote, "Indeed, being poor in a rich country may be more difficult to endure than being poor in a poor country, for the skills of surviving in poverty have largely been lost in America." Shipler's insights sparked my interest, and I started looking at the people I worked with a little differently. I became concerned especially about those who lacked the soft skills usually acquired through work. I began to wonder whether Americans have simply lost the "skills of surviving in poverty" because the vast amount of assistance programs available to them have eliminated the need to plan, prepare, think, and safeguard the survival of themselves and their families.

It started to seem to me that the loss of these skills is at least in part attributable to the loss of the feelings of pride and satisfaction that come with self-sufficiency. Some of my clients had no problem telling me straight out that their aim was to *avoid* working. For them, the rewards for not working seemed to surpass anything that might be gained from employment because, if they went to work, they would no longer be eligible for so many benefits. Some of the responses from clients that I've received when trying to encourage working over not working have left me speechless because, in essence, they're right about the loss of benefits that can occur as a result of gaining employment (see, for example, *How does welfare disincentivize work?* in my *Quora* entries). I started to wonder how we, as social service providers, could promote self-sufficiency while so many people would prefer to continue depending on our programs and services instead of getting a job.

Maybe I'm I being overly dramatic, but assistance programs could soon undergo a revamping that will leave those who have depended on them for generations scrambling for ways to survive. If these people lack the skills acquired through working, it is hard to see how they can maintain their households after social services have been significantly reduced or even eliminated. Given the financial situation in which the U.S. government finds itself, it appears that some of the funding that social services receive will eventually have to be redirected elsewhere. In particular, programs that have not produced the expected outcomes may end up on the chopping block. When I talked with my clients to assess their thought processes regarding what their next steps would be if their assistance were eliminated, I often received responses along the lines of "We'll deal with it when it happens." Should a reduction in assistance programs ever actually happen, we will see the extent to which they have diminished or eliminated the desire to work.

Simply put, then, we working people are tired of being punished for our efforts! We continue to contribute and *pay in* but are sometimes barely able to make it from month to month.

We watch our paychecks dissipate like smoke, with some of our earnings going to help fund programs that support those who have figured out how to work the system and pass that knowledge on to their children and grandchildren. However, the fact that families continue to receive social services for generations is pretty strong evidence that our programs are not working very well.

CHAPTER 4

Love at First Paycheck

When do we start to believe that working is necessary? I don't know about you, but it was love at first paycheck when I started working as a teenager. Something about that experience convinced me that I wanted paychecks to remain a part of my life until death did us part. My introduction to the world of work–beautifully orchestrated, I might add–was at the hands of my grandmother one summer. Believe me, after spending a lot of time at her house, I jumped at the chance to start working, if for no other reason than to avoid her list of grueling chores. Little did I know that I would fall head over heels in love with earning a paycheck.

That summer changed my life, starting with my grandmother's declaration that "You're not going to spend all day lounging around watching television just because school's out!" She informed me that our church was participating in a summer youth employment program made possible by the Comprehensive Employment and Training Act (CETA)[1] "You and the other young people in the church are getting jobs!" she explained.

"Lounging around"? I asked myself. *How can that be when she finds things for me to clean just out of spite?* At least that's how I felt about it. "Go soap down the lawn furniture and be sure to rinse it off, and take this steel wool to the barbecue grates!" she'd order. Heck, I already felt like the most berated, mistreated, tortured, forsaken, and despised kid who ever lived.

Getting a job-this was the first time I ever heard these words directed toward me, and I wasn't really sure how I felt about it. But how bad could working be? The only thing missing from the summers at my grandmother's house were bread and water rations and someone playing a harmonica off in the distance. All I knew was that working someplace else had to be better than working around the house and yard with "the warden" all summer long.

I still thought that all of this sounded suspicious and even downright underhanded. Still, I kept listening to her while, in my head, I imagined a gathering of cloaked grandmothers and mothers preparing all of us for the sacrifice. I could imagine them saying, "Those little crumb-snatchers are going to learn how to pull their own weight for a change, and they're buying their own school clothes this year too!"

In hindsight, that summer job not only gave me something productive to do but also kept me out of trouble. It was also a brilliant way to instill in me a strong work ethic and soft skills and to help me fall in love with earning money. So, my grandmother and I headed to the social security office to get the card that became a part of my life forever. I felt the excitement building as I waited for orientation day for my first job. I started on a Monday, and the work–if I really can call having such a cool job "working"–was one of the best, most fun, and most meaningful experiences in my life.

As it turned out, our jobs at the church as teenagers consisted of playing with and monitoring children while making sure that they stayed safe. We watched over these children from the community who attended the summer program as they participated in fun activities, received free lunches, and went on field trips, and we helped to keep them quiet during story time. We also assisted in the preparation of the children's lunches and chaperoned them on field trips to the zoo and museums and other educational settings. That was it, that was all we had to do, and they paid us for it–sweet!

This employment program was a godsend for the working parents who needed daycare for their children during the summer break as well as our families because we didn't spend the summer just hanging around. Instead, we learned how to work and earn our own money. I can still remember getting that envelope with my first paycheck in it, followed by a trip to the bank to open a savings account. If I remember correctly, that first paycheck, for two weeks of work, was for $69, but the important thing was that it was mine and I had earned it. I had had fun doing so and, in my mind, I was rich! They say that, if the first experience of doing something is positive, we tend to keep doing it and making money was something that I liked.

Some thirty years later, I experienced a moment of d*éjà vu* when I started working for a social service agency that had been awarded funding to create programs for low-income families. One of my assignments was to visit a local church that ran a summer program for teens: I had come full circle! Entering the church, I was directed to an enormous room full of young people around 14 to 18 years old. I saw from the looks on their faces that some of them were excited to be there while others seemed to have been enrolled in the program against their will–perhaps at the insistence of their grandmothers.

I instantly had a flash-back because they were being trained, as we had been, to be employees. That is, they were acquiring some of the tools and skills that they would need to fulfill their needs and desired as adults and that nobody would be able to take from them. As I had decades earlier, they were learning to work and be responsible while earning an income and (hopefully) having a blast doing it. My greatest hope was that they would grow to appreciate the relationship between working and earning a paycheck as much as I did.

I looked around at some of these young employees while waiting to speak with one of the supervisors, and I noticed at once that difference, that distinct *air* about some of them that went beyond their neat appearance and the style of their clothing. It was their attitude that suggested that these teens would go on to be anything that they wanted to be and have the kind of adult lives that they desired. They were being indoctrinated into the world of work, doing something meaningful that would pay off in the long run. These teens weren't sagging or slouching, and they smiled and greeted me with, "Yes, Ma'am" and "good morning."

I could tell just by looking at them that they came from families where manners were practiced and they thought twice before showing any attitude and did so rarely. And, when attitudes did raise their ugly heads, they probably were not tolerated. I imagined that these young people were probably also known by their parents' occupations and roles in the community ("she's Ms. So-and-so's daughter" or "that's Mr. So-and-so's son"). They acquired admirable attributes from the environment as they grew up. Don't get me wrong, a few teens were, "lying low," apparently hoping to go undetected as they remained idle. Even so, at least they were involved in this program and not out in the street getting into trouble. There were many other places where these young people might have been, but they were in this church, learning what it means to work and get paid.

I find it interesting to talk to people about almost anything. During school visits, I met various staff members, from principals to members of the custodial crews. I befriended one gentleman who was a school janitor. He had retired from the military, and he shared with me that retirement had almost driven him insane, so he had picked up employment at the school for something to do. We would talk about various things during my visits and, one day, I asked him whether he thought there would ever be another draft. He replied, "Nah, that's what registering with Selective Service is for; they'll pull enlistees from there."

While I was talking with him, I was thinking about a job that I had helping young men secure employment. Before I could start working with them, I had to make sure that those who were more than 17 years old were registered with Selective Service. I was pretty sure that the high schools took care of registering their 18-year-old male students, but I worked with high-risk adolescents who had dropped out of school and were walking the streets all day. Some of them had kids of their own while still being kids themselves.

Several of these young people had already become caught up in the legal system. One of them even gleamed when he told me that, when he landed in both the county jail and prison, it was like a family reunion because two of his brothers, an uncle, and a few cousins were there, too. Acceptance into a program such as the one that employed me was favorable in the eyes of probation officers, especially when the probationers were paid, because they had no jobs. My activities kept them off of the streets for a little while, and were able to help them gain permanent employment in the community just by being involved in our program. For those who had felony convictions, our program was a plus because, again, they hadn't been successful in obtaining jobs on their own.

When I asked my retired serviceman/school-worker friend whether there would be another draft, I was thinking about the young people who walk the streets every day with no employment or even the desire to find a job, including some whom I had worked with in the past. As I mentioned, they had dropped out of school at an early age and, therefore, were not registered with the Selective Service at school. This consideration prompted me to think that it would be a good deterrent for those who are troubled but have not been in sufficient trouble to be incarcerated yet if word got out that going before a judge could result in being sentenced to military service; it could change things.

First-time offenders could complete two-weeks of military-style training so that they would be prepared for combat on the front lines as soon as possible. In most cases, the anger is already in them, and the energy is surely there to get out and fight and possibly kill someone. These troubled young people are not receiving any form of discipline anywhere else, and a great many of them are homeless, just bouncing from place to place and going wherever they can. In my opinion, this approach would be more effective in reducing the number of young people who continue to commit crimes than going to prison, which is clearly not the deterrent that it once was. The prospect of being shipped off to serve could change some minds about committing crimes even more than the three-strike law.[2]

Those who are already in prison, on the other hand, could be given the option of early release providing that they go straight to the front-line training. Some of them have something to prove, so the drive is already in them. After the training, they could be shipped off to join those already on the front lines of defense. This approach would also be cost-effective, for correctional facilities in this country spend an average of $45,771 to care for an inmate for one year according to a recent estimate. [3] I only mention this military option because I don't hear about boot camps anymore. I don't even know whether they still exist after the budget cuts over the years.

I was told many years ago when I was contacting recruiters in the effort to help the young men I was working with that the military no longer accepts high school drop-outs and prefers recruits who have completed at least a year of college. I also believe that they no longer accept anyone who has a criminal record, as they did when I was a kid. If my memory serves me well, enlisting in the military 45 or 50 years ago could wipe a criminal record clean. As a matter of fact, back then, parents often took sons who were headed for trouble and already had misdemeanor records to recruiters' offices to scare them straight before it was too late. This course of action by parents was effective. As I have personally seen, military discipline, or the threat of it, often represents the best choice for parents trying to set their teenage sons on the right path.

In some places, crime is increasing, including homicide, aggravated assault, robbery, property crimes, and so on. When the consequences of serious crime are not severe, offenders who have no fear and possess survival or combat skills learned from living on the streets pose a menace to public service workers. In any case, folks in the United States want to see their streets cleaned up and remaining clean.

So, what's the point of all this? At the beginning of this chapter, I asked, *when do some of us start to believe that work is necessary?* Now I'll ask, *when do others of us start to believe that working is* not *necessary–and what puts people on one path or the other?* My experience and observations have led me to believe that most people think working is necessary to survive but some don't. Some of the individuals I provided services for have proven that working is not always necessary and they have avoided doing so for many years. The position that I held involved disbursing funding that had been awarded to create programs for low-income families. I learned that those who were *not working*–among whom numbered most of the population that we served–were still being paid in one way or another in that they were receiving our services. Whether in the form of cash, food, clothing, gasoline, or utility payments, we were providing benefits that helped them survive.

When it came to the work programs and job placement opportunities that were a big part of our responsibility, it was my experience that not everyone wanted to take advantage of what we had to offer. Some would look like I insulted them when it came to identifying suitable employment opportunities. Much to my chagrin, I found that a good percentage, approximately 60%, of the individuals would rather *not* be placed in employment. They argued that they would lose too much if they went to work, and, after they presented me with the figures, I usually had to admit that they were right. This realization would make for a tough day at the office. When they said, "I'll lose my food stamps" or "I won't qualify for the heating assistance program in the winter" (which would save them $1,100 out of pocket every winter, not counting what they would lose during the summer months-another $300), I realized that it would be almost impossible to persuade them to give all of it up and go to work.

This is what we're seeing now: the need to encourage people to work instead of not working. The pandemic caused business closures, the loss of jobs and left many unable to pay the bills. However, it also resulted in stimulus payments, increases in unemployment payouts and food stamp benefits, and deferred rent payments. When household incomes increased in one way or another, we saw families who had never or only rarely had to apply for unemployment or any other form of assistance receive more for being out of work than they took in when working.

As a result, families whose members I knew personally were out of work and were able to do better than they did when they were employed. They had money left over and were able to pay all of their bills, especially when they didn't have to make rent payments (I know the questions that you probably have after what I just said, and I have the same ones). I visited one of my friends who received full low-income benefits, and she had three freezers full of food because of the doubling of her food stamp allowances starting in March 2020. Her new chest and an upright freezer were purchased with her stimulus money. Once accustomed to the extra income and benefits as a result of the stimulus money and other perks, families were able to rethink their way of living, their careers, and their futures.

In my opinion, those who have taken a hiatus from working as a result of Covid-19 have had the opportunity to experience what it's like to live better without having to work to work to do so—just like low-income families that have been receiving full benefits for years. The difference is that those idled by the pandemic are used to working and thus have a greater propensity to seek employment when they can. So, when we see businesses having a hard time finding employees or people choosing not to work who have always done so in the past, I think that they may simply be taking a time-out to reflect on their lives while living off of the assistance that their tax dollars have been funding for so long.

CHAPTER 5

Plates as Big as States

"Feel what it's like to truly starve, and I guarantee that you'll forever think twice before wasting food."
Criss Jami, Killosophy

During what feels like 100 years of my working life, a young Kenyan student at one point taught me something that I will never forget. We were employed at a university, in food service, and he was helping me prepare the vegetables for the next meal. I was cleaning celery and disposing of the leafy parts. He asked me why, and I said, "Because we don't use that part of the celery stalk." "In my country," he replied in his rich Kenyan accent, "we use all of the vegetables when we prepare meals. One of the reasons we are so excited about being accepted at universities in the United States is because you have so much here that you can afford to throw things away". That young man had no idea how profound an impact his words that day have had in my life in everything that I do.

It's a doubled-edged sword to be viewed by other countries as a place so rich that we can afford to be wasteful. Or can we? I have worked with clients who receive public assistance from the state and government, so I know how much they receive monthly and the additional assistance provided to them at the time of this writing. I found myself wondering whether a family of five really consumes $762 worth of groceries per month, a family of six consumes $914 worth, a family of seven consumes $1,011 per month, and a family of eight consumes $1,155 worth.[1]

I know I said that this book wouldn't include statistics or numbers, but I'm breaking my promise just this once or maybe twice. For some reason, I just don't think that the heads of households, working heads of households that is, with families just above the poverty line, spend that much on groceries, but I could be mistaken. Of course these days, it's not only possible, it's probable. What I do know is that someone somewhere calculated the recommended amount of monthly grocery assistance to meet the needs of each household. You may be thinking, "Of course it takes that much; that's nothing when it comes to purchasing groceries. Get over yourself!"

By comparison, an acquaintance of mine has a retired grandmother who is only eligible for $13 per month in food stamps. I heard this acquaintance say, "And they expect that to buy enough groceries for her for the month?" But then, those of us who are consumed with just trying to make it to work every day may not have the time to think about how much free food assistance other families receive. On payday, we folks who are working and barely getting by may simply be fixated on how, after we have paid the bills, our last $40 will get us through the next two weeks.

Observations such as food stamp amounts, sufficient or not, bring me to the main point of this chapter. On a weekly basis, at my side hustle, I often saw food being thrown away, either because someone had already eaten it once that week, or just out of habit, or because the food was free. This is purely based on my observations and isn't meant to be taken personally. I'm not saying that everyone throws away food; just that I have seen a lot of food waste at some of the places I've worked.

As a Segway, I catch myself thinking several times a day, based on where I am or what I'm doing, "Now, that is an interesting study for a thesis or dissertation", and in this instance, studies are being conducted regarding food waste [2,3,4], but within research there is still more research to be done. I mean, if they can conduct studies on the number of people who don't wash their hands after bathroom visits, why not do more studies on food wastefulness? (See what happens when you've been in school too long?)

Lately, what catches my attention are television commercials that show how communities and restaurants, especially those that have had to close for a time because of the pandemic, have started coming together and finding creative ways to use food that would otherwise have been wasted. Community refrigerators and food boxes to feed the poor, homeless, or displaced have become even more useful, and that's a good thing. Establishments and organizations that are supplying repurposed food items merit all manner of support, especially funding.

So, you may be thinking, as I once did, that anyone who earns a low income can get food stamps, which means that no one should be hungry. I say the same thing about children living in low-income households, yet we hear and see so many stories that some children are indeed hungry. I have heard the same thing working with teachers, and there's just no excuse for such a situation in a wealthy country.

I once taught sociology which is the study of human social relationships and institutions. The subject matter is diverse, ranging from crime to religion, from the family to the state, from the divisions of race and social class to the shared beliefs of a common culture, and from social stability to radical change across whole societies. Sociology brings together the study of these diverse subjects to explain how human action and consciousness both shape and are shaped by surrounding cultural and social structures.[5] That may seem like a lot to retain, but the perspective of sociology informs the way in which portions of this book play out.

That said, I've always found the study of people, cultures, and beliefs to be very interesting. As I observe individuals' habits, mannerisms, dialects, movements, and speech, I always wonder what experiences, from birth to adulthood, have had the most impact on them. Now I work with clients who depend on public assistance in order to live, something that is unfortunately becoming increasingly common. Because I have a bit of an inquisitive nature, I can't help but notice what people are buying when I'm in grocery stores, and I know that I'm not the only one. I sometimes think that the people we assist with food stamps may not realize how truly fortunate they are to be able to eat so well and how supportive our county is of those who are in need.

When I go to the grocery store to buy a couple of items, I'd see other customers with prime cuts of meat in their grocery carts, the kind that I would imagine are served at a Waldorf Astoria (and I honestly intend both to dine and to lodge at one before I leave this planet: I *do* set goals). It would be sort of funny because I would have flash backs to the times that I worked in food service, the main concern was always how much money was spent to purchase meat. Seeing grocery carts filled to capacity, I would shift from one foot to the other wondering which line I can get through with my couple of items fastest because I was usually on my lunch break and didn't have all day to wait.

Back to my main theme: I secured a part-time job, my side hustle, to go along with my full-time job because I needed the money. Since I have to pay working folks' prices–full prices for necessities like rent, utilities, and groceries, the paycheck from my full-time job just wasn't enough. The irony is, working folks are exerting the expected effort plus some, but we still have to budget our money just to put food on the table. Our grocery carts are not so full; it almost feels like we're being punished for working.

At the part-time job, I get a chance to see the intimate side of clients who receive public assistance. And when I say intimate, I mean *cooking*. I get the opportunity to watch meals being prepared and consumed-thus *plates as big as states*. One day, I watched a box of macaroni being prepared with an entire stick of margarine plopped into the hot pasta and cheese sauce. The package calls for three tablespoons, which is less than half a stick. Next, I noticed a half-gallon storage bag full of flour being tossed in the trash after a little of it was used to coat some pork chops. Perhaps the young lady used so much to prepare her meal because she could, because it was there, and because it was free.

If I seem harsh and judgmental, I'm not because this young lady, age twenty-two or so, had no idea that she didn't have to use that much to prepare a meal. She never even had to think about it because free food had always been there for her in abundance. She and her children were probably not the first generation in her family to live on public assistance. When she was done cooking that day, she filled the plates, piling hers with what looked like enough to feed a small village. I guess the look on my face didn't hide what I was thinking at the time, because she said, "I made too much, didn't I? I can eat some of it for lunch tomorrow, I guess." I thought to myself, "You could eat some of it for the rest of the week!"

Shame on me, and hail to the super-size mega meals that we have grown so accustomed to. She is only a product of plenty, a sign of the good fortune that our country enjoys. But there is the other side, those who seduce a portion of the population into believing that the overabundance of food and free money is a right. It's as if it's a gift for just being born and breathing based on the premise–which I hear, pretty much on a daily basis–"whether I worked for it or not, I deserve it because I signed up for it." That's pretty much the way it is now, whether working folks like it or not.

And, speaking of food, as it relates to the topic of this chapter, a couple of my former jobs required that I conduct home visits. One particular day jammed-packed with home visits, I visited a small town with a little grocery store. As I wound up my visits for the day, I stopped in for a cold fruit juice to drink on the way back to the office. My eyes instinctively zoomed in on some of the prices indicated on the shelves, which held limited choices of food items and some household items since it was just a little country store.

I realized that the items on which my eyes randomly landed were priced 5 to 15 cents higher than they would have been at a major grocery store, including my fruit drink. My complaining as I crossed the parking lot was loud enough for a gentleman who was getting out of his car to hear me. He said with a bashful grin, "This is the only store for seven miles, and most of the folks around here are on food stamps, so it's not like they're paying out any *money* for it." Well, I thought all the way home, I guess he's right. If people in a small town don't have transportation, and they don't have to pay money for their groceries, then I was making a bigger deal about the cost of the items in the store than I should have been. In that instance, the extra 5 to 15 cents doesn't hurt for either the customer or the grocery store owner. Needless to say, I made that overpriced fruit juice last as long as I could because it wasn't a gift just for me being me–paying hard-earned cash for it made it matter.

Years later, I found myself in another grocery store (not much of a life, right?) where I heard a conversation that was so funny it took everything I had not to roll on the floor laughing. As her groceries were making their way down the conveyer belt, the woman in front of me said that she had made it a point to shop that day because she had heard on the news that the cost of food was going up the next day. I felt it coming; my knees started feeling weak, and I was trying to keep a straight face, but my mind said "Wait for it... booyah!" and out pops the blue food stamp card. I realize that, these days, unfortunately, we're all watching our spending, but really? Can you imagine how much more her statement would have meant if she had been paying cash for her groceries?

Sometimes, I seem to live in a world that makes no sense at all. Up is down, down is up, and I'm so confused. I see and hear public service announcements suggesting that there is just not enough food to go around, especially when it comes to feeding children. However, I know of many resources that supply food almost on a daily basis, though I sometimes wonder whether anyone else realizes this. Depending on their income, many families qualify not only for food stamps but, also for access to food banks including the mobile food banks run by some churches.

A year or so ago, I saw a convenience store marquee reading, "Need Food? Call 555-1212". I've participated in numerous summer food programs for youths, in particular, the free or reduced breakfast and lunch programs at area schools. I saw a religious broadcast a while back about a church that provided weekend food packages so that children have something to eat on days when school wasn't in session. Some schools provide this service too. There are also WIC programs for children and even soup kitchens in some areas. As of late, community refrigerators and donated food boxes are becoming increasingly more valuable.

With all of these available food resources, there are a couple of things that I still can't seem to figure out. To begin with, if families qualify for food stamps (at the amounts listed earlier in this chapter), and there are so many other services that also provide food, why are we seeing hungry people-especially children, since most of these services were established out of concern that children are not getting enough to eat? What's happening to all of that assistance? With the swipe of a card, it's abracadabra and there's food, so why do I keep hearing that many people who live in the United States don't have enough of it? Heads of households have shared with me that they still have purchasing power left at the end of the month on their EBT (Electronic Benefit Transfer) cards, so what's the deal?

As I mentioned, my job responsibilities have included offering services that encourage self-sufficiency and independence. The outcome, if successful, is a reduction in the number of families receiving public assistance benefits. And, as I have continued to preach on a daily basis, a good number of public assistance programs may eventually be on their way out. At the time of this writing, the funds paid in, that small amount of workers' tax dollars, are not enough to keep up with the growing number of families signing up to receive food stamps.

I had the privilege once to teach a class for young mothers on ways to stretch their income and food resources. We have to provide services for a given number of individuals and families in order to keep operating and to keep our jobs. Some of the services that agencies provide mandate attendance, requiring participation in adult education in exchange for whatever *goodies* the clients come to us to receive. It's sort of a way to foster some responsibility.

Of course, life would be so much easier if everything was just given freely with no effort required on the part of the recipient. If the folks we serve didn't have to meet with us or attend classes that some of them couldn't care less about, they could just live their lives without us having to *bother* them, and we would be liked a little more. On the other hand, if we didn't teach these classes, we wouldn't have jobs, and then we, too, would have all of the free time in the world to complain about having to attend a class.

The disdain is written all over some clients' faces because they are being *made* to sit in the classes in order to get what they want. All that we are trying to do is to teach them how to make their groceries and other purchases go further. We are trying to show them how to purchase items that can be used to make more than one meal. For some of those in attendance, though, our helpful tips are simply of no interest. Their mindset appeared to be the same as those who I saw throwing away lots of food, or, I'd hear them say that they didn't have to learn anything about meal planning.

Before I started a class, I would sometimes have a Rodney Dangerfield moment (pulling at my collar and thinking, "Tough crowd, I tell ya!"), but, usually, by halfway through, we're all having a good time—I like my courses to be comfortable, fun, and funny. The only time that this familiar foreboding doom is absent is when I'm teaching children since they don't have the mindset of "Just give me what I want so I can get out of here!"

One day, I was teaching a class on money-saving tips, including making the most of coupons, something that I was pretty excited about. All that I can say is, thank God there were a few women in the class who actually engaged in *couponing* since the rest of the class couldn't have cared less. One woman shared that she worked part-time and her husband worked full-time, they were buying a house, and, with three children, their combined paychecks just weren't enough. So, she signed up for the assistance program, and, she said, usually saved around $170 per month thanks to coupons. Another woman, a single mother, said that she saved around $60 per month using coupons, savings that she put toward her heating bills in the winter.

In an attempt to engage with all of these ladies, I went around the room and asked each for any input they had about their experience using coupons-and I saw her! She was a young mother, maybe nineteen years old, pregnant and with a toddler. She glared at me with an "I hate you!" look when I called on her and she announced that she didn't and wouldn't use coupons. I had come across attitudes like hers often enough and already had an idea that the rest of her answers, if she chose to participate at all, would be just as warm and fuzzy. So, I couldn't wait to move on to the next part of the class and enjoy more of her abuse.

I then asked the women for examples of ways to save money. One mother shared that she paid careful attention to the portions of meat that she served having planned out her family's menus before going to the grocery store. For example, she would buy enough ground beef for three meals (specifically, hamburgers, chili, and meatloaf). This was something our grandmothers and our mothers did out of necessity.

I remembered my mother scolding me when I was a kid, saying, usually about chips or cookies "Don't sit there and eat all of that at once! They have to last us until next payday!" I remember my grandmother telling me that, when she was a teenager during the Depression, she and her friends would walk to the diner and ask for a cup of hot water and some crackers. Then they would pour some of the catsup that was on the counter into their cups to make a kind of tomato soup-ewww! Though I still wanted to devour all of the chips and cookies in one sitting, I would recall my grandmother's story about that tomato soup and decide to save some for another day. I still shudder at that flash-back, but now it makes perfect sense.

I returned to the sullen young lady and asked her how she prepared meals. You would have thought that I'd just thrown holy water on Linda Blair (those of you who weren't around in the 1970s, can Google that). That brown-haired, blue-eyed beauty spat back that she didn't think about it and bought whatever she needed and was done with it. As if the sting I felt wasn't painful enough, I went on to ask what she did with the leftovers. "We don't eat leftovers!" she snapped. "We eat it once and the rest goes in the trash!"

At least she didn't ask how much longer the class was going to last. But there you have it: throw it in the trash and don't worry about tomorrow, or the next meal for that matter, because there's plenty, and it's all there just for the asking and taking.

CHAPTER 6

So Humbly Sad to Meet You

I decided to write this chapter immediately after "Plates as Big as States" because there may come a time when the availability of food and other life-sustaining necessities grows limited. As a matter of fact, we're starting to see this now. Such a turn of events would be devastating for those who depend on receiving public assistance services, and even more so for those who have recently and unexpectedly found themselves in need of assistance owing to circumstances such as the pandemic. In my area, friend of mine whose food stamp allotment had doubled over the spring and summer to more than $600 per month for her family of three, fell to a mere $14.

It appeared that the Pandemic Food Stamp/Supplemental Nutritional Assistance Program (P-SNAP) would be ending. It had been providing the maximum amount plus an additional amount of $95 (15%) per month per household.[1] The Pandemic Emergency Unemployment Compensation had been scheduled to end when I started writing this portion of this chapter; it too had been extended. The emergency and extra assistance was a godsend for everyone who received it, especially working-class families, but, through it all, I found myself asking first, "Where is all of the money coming from to fund the emergency assistance, maybe partly from FEMA funding?" Second, I asked, "How long will the emergency assistance last?" Lastly, I asked, "How are they going to recoup the funds that helped us through the various crises?"

These thoughts took me back to the late 1980s, when grant-funded programs were facing severe budget cuts that often left professional positions in human services and related fields empty and unfillable. We were on pins and needles during that time, constantly wondering whether we would be among those caught up in the next wave of lay-offs. We also dreaded the extra caseloads because of the job cuts, especially since we were already having a hard time keeping up with the work. Budget cuts were necessary because the funding was either reduced or cut entirely. The situation now makes me wonder whether future cuts will have to happen again to replenish emergency funds that have been used in various other crises.

I do have the sense that, should decisions have to be made again about what to fund and what not to fund, this time, consideration may be given to the length and number of times households have received public assistance. That is, the time may come when families have reached the limit on services as long-term or generational recipients of public assistance. A limit could easily be imposed on the number of times households have received public assistance in one form or another. My reasoning in this regard is that, if a "spam risk" caller can monitor every time I end a call and then call me immediately afterward, monitoring the number of times that applicants have received public assistance should be a piece of cake.

For those who work in public assistance, it's just part of our training to ask questions when applicants apply for services and we see social security numbers showing up in different or multiple households. For instance, it's not uncommon to see Mary Ann living in one household but appearing to live in another as well. Sometimes, the system provides easy answers to our questions, but, other times, it's obvious that the answers are being made up as we go along. Of course, there have been attempts to impose limits on some forms of public assistance for example, reducing provisions from 60 months to 45 months[2], but they do not seem to have had any real effect when it comes to the expectancy outcomes for repeat public assistance applicants.

Now, we're seeing individuals and families who have lost employment and for the first time, or for one of only a few times, have had to apply for assistance.

They're in need of help but somehow unable to receive it. This is very sad and unfortunate because these individuals and families are the ones, in the words of the title of this chapter, I am so humbly sad to meet. We are painfully turning them away when they contact us for assistance because the assistance that they need has already been used up by those who receive it repeatedly—and I mean like clockwork. Clients who receive assistance month after month and year after year have come to depend on these programs to meet their needs. They consider making it on their own the last possible resort and come to us first—the opposite of how things are supposed to be.

It's the same no matter the need or agencies involved. Some applicants asking for assistance already know when the funds will become available and, in some cases, how much they're entitled to (see "Strategies: CEOs and Millionaires Could Learn a Thing or Two"). I field questions such as, "Should I go ahead and pay this bill or do you all have money?" Once, I overheard a woman call her uncle to ask whether he had already paid a bill. "Well, don't," she said, "because the state funds have arrived." Situations like this make me wonder whether I'm working for those who are truly in need.

For the less-experienced applicants, though—those who are unfamiliar with and don't use assistance programs regularly or have decided to exhaust every other means before asking for help often arrive too late. Worse yet, when they finally do break down and come to us, and there's still assistance dollars left, they don't qualify, mainly because they have remained employed. These "left out" individuals and families are the seniors, the farmers, the essential workers who accept the employment that many of my clients reject, those who have worked for companies, sometimes for 20 or more years, that have had to close their doors for good.

So, we can't seem to help the applicants who would rather jump in front of trains than ask for help, and, when they do come to us, we have nothing for them. They're not used to applying for assistance and usually don't even know how. I can sense their sadness when they walk through the door, sometimes so burdened and exhausted from worrying about how they are going to make ends meet that they find it difficult even to hold their heads up. They seem to feel that they have failed their families and themselves. So humble and so broken are they that I believe them when they tell me that they have never asked for public assistance. Indeed, it's obvious that they haven't because they avoid eye contact, and their tears don't magically dry up as soon as I start phoning around to find a nook or a cranny that I haven't searched yet for a crumb of assistance for them. I hear it in their voices, which are filled with fear, as if they are lost and sliding off an icy road in the dark genuine fear, helplessness, and distress.

I will always remember meeting with a woman whom someone drove into town so that she could come to us for help. She was in her seventies and appeared frail, but she had been known to cut her own wood to burn for heat in the past. Using wood for heat is something that I'd have to look up on YouTube to learn how to do without burning down the house. She lived in the country, and I got the feeling that she could take care of herself if she had to (think Granny Clampett). She needed wood delivered to her home because she was running out, but our funds were gone, and I had nothing to tell her. She reached for my hand with her trembling hands and frail fingers and, through tears, asked, "What am I going to do?" Since there was no assistance money left, all that I had were the stammered words and unimaginative suggestions that became the script that we all recited once the state funds ran out.

This is what I struggle with: these are the people who deserve first dibs when it comes to receiving any form of assistance because they have worked and earned the right: they've paid their dues. These are *not* the folks who wave me off to work in the morning sitting under a tree and are sitting in the same spot when I return in the evening. They are *not* the folks I work every day to support. No, the people who touch my heart are those who have found themselves laid off or have otherwise encountered legitimately hard times, the folks who are truly being punished for working. These clients, I'm pretty sure, I will never see again after I have helped them once because reaching out for public assistance has been such a shock that they will do anything to avoid asking for help again. No, I won't be seeing them again next month and the month after that or whenever it's "sign-up" time again.

Somehow, we've mixed things up. It seems that we are—unintentionally, *I hope*— encouraging dependence on assistance programs instead of directing people away from them. This is why the same families show up in the system for 5, 10, 15, and more years. I say "I hope" because, if the recipients of generational public assistance understood that there has been a tendency to make it easy for them to become dependent, and in some instances almost addicted to assistance programs instead of encouraging them to develop their strengths, they wouldn't be so quick to accept this kind of fix. Reenrollment limits could discourage individuals and families from returning to us over and over again–teach them to fish rather than giving them fish, as the saying goes. Once they have maxed out, they're done!

I have tried to preach to the clients who come to us over and over again, that, by surrendering their families' wellbeing to a program, to *the system*, they acknowledge that they cannot survive on their own. The path of least resistance–applying for assistance–is popular because, of course, it's easy. Recipients only need to come in to sign up twice a year for utility bill payments and then once a year or every other year, when the food stamps office asks for a re-up; then, they can glide through the rest of the year worry-free. I am shaking my head as I say this because even committing to do what is necessary to receive the *free assistance* is still sometimes a struggle. "Just keep your appointments," I'd tell them, and then, when they missed their appointments and fail to reschedule, I would find myself thinking, "You had only one thing to do!"

In our area, low-income households could receive up to $1,400 a year from the state for their utility bills, thus freeing up the money for something else. We folks, who don't qualify, mainly because we work, may have to sit in the cold and dark if there's no freeze order in effect. When it comes to us, though, the working poor[3] low income and unemployed folks seem to think, "You're working, so how can you run short on cash to pay the bills?" Well the reason is that working folks, as well as recently unemployed folks, have full-price lives. There are no discounts, no reduced-price or "free" utilities or meals or other things in our everyday lives.

Our income, when we find ourselves in a bind, prevents us from receiving free assistance, so most of us don't even think about applying for help. "Go get a loan," some might say, but that means more expense and digging a deeper hole to climb out of in the future. We have full-price lives, and, as we're now seeing on the news every day because of the pandemic, we're standing in lines or sitting in cars in lines with others like us hoping to get some relief for our families. Working folks who have never had to ask for help before in their lives are now seeking it but there doesn't seem to be any there for them. There are more people who don't qualify for food stamps because of their income from the past six months (prior to being laid off) standing in lines for food than I would have ever imagined. They're hungry, too, but, because they worked, they are above the poverty line and are turned away–ain't that a kick in the head?

For those recipients who know what's out there and could write a book on how to live for free, the concern is, "What are you giving away today and how much of it can I get?" There are so many ways in which families that have not been involved in the system before could receive help rather than being met with a sad "sorry," as has happened during the pandemic. I said at the beginning of this book that I would offer some suggestions and solutions to problems that I encountered working in the field. In instances such as those that I just mentioned–families that on paper are above the poverty line but have lost their main sources of income—it is just a matter of looking at work histories and last dates of employment. The same process used in filing for unemployment could identify the families that, in my opinion, deserve to be at the front of the line or moved to quicker lines than those for the families that have often received the assistance. The process has failed to take into account the waiting period before a recently unemployed worker receives any financial support. In the meantime, the bills keep piling up. "We're all just one missed paycheck away from poverty," as the saying goes.

The clients I worked with were required to submit the bills that they needed to pay along with proof of work income or public assistance. The latter automatically qualified them to have their bills covered whereas proof of income from working most times eliminated this possibility—this needs to be reevaluated. At the start of the pandemic, this same process could have moved those who do not regularly receive assistance to the front of the line for a change. Errors made during the pandemic will, hopefully, recognize and motivate some changes so as to distinguish those who have made careers out of participating in assistance programs from those asking for help for the first time. Hopefully, changes will take place in the system so as to promote and support the members of the working class who find themselves in a crisis so that they, too, receive the relief that they ask for.

Of course, people who are working may have savings, but there is not always money left over at the end of the month for them. Many Americans have been struggling to pay their bills and unable to save much if anything during the prolonged period of tepid wage growth and the rising cost of living in recent years. According to recent report, 54% of U.S. people (125 million adults) were living paycheck-to-paycheck, of whom 21% were struggling to pay their bills, leaving little or no money left after spending on necessities.[4]

For years, money has continually gone into public assistance programs. I know that there are employee savings plans for use in the distant future, but couldn't state and government agencies look into saving plans tied to wages? For instance, if an employee earns $15 per hour, the state or federal government could deposit $2 into a savings plan earmarked specifically for the employee's use in the event of a valid emergency or crisis. There are so many policies that could help those who remain employed rather than relying on assistance programs; the sky's the limit. Next, those whose names and social security numbers appear to be in just about every system there is need to be identified–because, yes, identity theft was an issue for some of my clients.

The funding to create new social service positions to track identity theft as well as identify double-dippers would be repaid many times over by reducing the number of individuals who are being claimed as the recipients of benefits from more than one pot. In my experience, some families were well aware of the *extra people* listed as members of their households. Once I started asking questions I would hear, "Oh yeah, well, no, that person doesn't live with us anymore." Then, I would ask, "For how long?" I would hear, "Oh, not for a long time." Next, I would ask, "So, why didn't you make that change on your last application?" and

I would hear crickets. Here's the scary part: because we have doled out the goods so generously for so long, should we ever exhaust all of our resources, or should programs ever be eliminated, a great many people would be at a loss because they have never had to fend for themselves thanks to the assistance programs that have always been there for them.

The nice publisher man, after listening to my account of some of the problems that, I feel, our public assistance programs have caused, said that he would like to see some of the solutions for these problems in this book, just as I promised at the beginning. The pandemic made the plight of working people in the U.S. plainly visible. I have a feeling that, during this coming decade if not sooner, changes will start to happen because our efforts thus far have not been effective. A possible solution, then, is to do as I have suggested and arrange the system so that those who have never or only rarely received public assistance move to the front of the line for a change. Those who have been living for years on assistance programs could move to the back of the line at least until people in positions like mine no longer have clients who make us feel that we should be saying, "I'm so humbly sad to meet you…again!"

CHAPTER 7

Hail that Ambulance! My Doctors Don't Cost a Thing

Excruciating that was the level of pain I was in and had been for quite some time. I was armed with a topical dental analgesic (ibuprofen) and, as a backup; I also had pure vanilla extract sitting on my desk for easy access. I had a horrible toothache and hoped that, just as unexpectedly as it started, it would go away again. Thinking back, I remembered that in my early twenties, I didn't have any dental issues. In fact, it seemed that I didn't start to have problems like this until I was working for companies that offered dental insurance. Almost every time I went to the dentist after I had insurance, I heard nothing but bad news—things kept getting worse, or at least that's what I thought. So, to avoid hearing more bad news, I simply put off going to the dentist until the pain was so severe that I considered jumping in front of a Mack truck for relief.

"So, just go to the dentist!" someone might say. Well, doing so would make sense, but this chapter will make clear why, sometimes, as a working woman, that wasn't my first choice. Ideally, you work, and, hopefully, you have a job that offers health benefits, and, hopefully, the deductible is low enough that you can actually schedule an appointment to see your doctor, dentist, or some other practitioner. Therein lies the problem for many working folks: it isn't always easy to seek care because many factors have to be considered, leaving an office visit as the absolute last resort. Other considerations include interruptions of a worker's daily routine and previous obligations (family and work), even for those who happen to have on hand, or at least to have access to, the funds needed just to walk through the door (i.e., the co-payments).

So, back to my desk covered with pain medicine. I have had two clients who I remember because of their especially beautiful teeth. I've seen perfect pearly whites on celebrities, but having them right in front of me—wow! So I asked them about their smiles and the names of their dentists. I received the same answer: their dentists worked at clinics for low-income patients. On other occasions as well, I heard people remark on the high quality of the dentists at practices that only admitted the patients whose income fell below a certain threshold.

The woman with the first of these beautiful smiles was so proud of hers that, after I complimented her, she told me which dentist to ask for and declared,

"It only took two visits, and Medicaid paid, so I didn't have to pay a thing!" At first, I thought that she had her natural teeth, but, as we talked, I learned that they were not. She had received a full set of dentures free of charge. The second woman, with beautiful teeth told me the same thing: her office visits and new teeth hadn't cost her a thing thanks to Medicaid.

This brings me to my main point. It's likely that neither of the women had to be in pain for very long or wait long for an appointment. They could just walk in, and, since they had probably been there before, all of the information about their income (or lack thereof) was probably already in the system. Neither of the women would have had to come up with any money in order to have access to their practitioners. They came to my office because they were signing up (again) to receive public assistance therefore, were not working. Their daily routines afforded them the time to visit a dentist without having to juggle many other commitments. They may have needed to secure transportation to the clinics where they received treatment, but major or numerous changes were probably much less of an issue had they been employed. So, I couldn't help thinking how nice it must feel to be unemployed and still have the prettiest teeth and all for free, at that! It's my impression that a beautiful smile can be beneficial in securing employment—if securing employment is the goal, that is.

Examples such as these make it seem as if people are better off being eligible for low-income services or being on or remaining on public assistance than work. As a result, it can be tough for social service workers to convince our clients to trade public assistance for a job. Doing so seems absurd to them when the income from employment can end their eligibility for free services, including Medicaid.

As an experiment, I decided to give the dental facility where my clients received their perfect teeth a call. I wanted to compare prices, find out what I needed to do to schedule an appointment, and so on. The woman I spoke with informed me that, if I didn't have Medicaid or Medicare, I would need to bring in my pay stubs or tax returns. She asked for my dental insurance information and the amount of my bi-weekly gross income. After putting me on a hold briefly, she picked up the phone again and told me that I would need to bring in approximately $150 because I hadn't used my insurance that year so nothing had yet been applied toward my deductible. I would need to bring in cash, a check, or my bank card–great!

To continue my experiment, and since I already had her on the phone, I asked, "So, what if I wasn't working, and I didn't have Medicaid or Medicare, and I had no insurance?" She explained that I would need to bring in my latest tax return and would probably have to pay the full amount of the dental procedure that I needed, which was $2,000. I would be considered low or no income, but, if I hadn't signed up for public assistance and food stamps, and depending on what my tax return showed, I might not be considered for the sliding scale fee that they sometimes offered either. In essence, because I chose to work, I was just hung out to dry, sore tooth and all.

If I had incorporated this real-life scenario into my "pitch" to get my clients working, they would have thought that I had taken leave of my senses. They had already figured out that, as I was just saying, if they started working, they could be punished for it in terms of losing most of what they received when they were not working. Too many "out-of-pocket" dollars would be expected to be paid for necessities if they were to join the workforce so why bother? Workforce programs have been trying to get most if not all of the clients who sign up for free services employed since inception. Don't get me wrong there are some individuals who, rather than having to be in constant contact with us and listen to us, would prefer to get off of assistance, and I applaud them!

"So, what's this all about anyway?" you ask. Don't worry; it'll all come together when we *hail ambulances*. My duties as a "motivator to employment" included making sure that all of the paperwork was signed, dated, and submitted in a timely manner. Usually, this task was impossible; it felt like running fast but getting nowhere. This situation could explain the high turnover rate in this field. Of course, there are workers who have provided services for a long time and learned how to go through the motions: just stamp 'em through, "see you next time," and get paid. They look at the "revolving door" thing as job security.

Part of our work week consisted of "chasing" clients who were not living up to their end of the agreement. And when this happened, which was every day; my thoughts were why sign up for services if there was no intention to do what was initially agreed upon. They received what they wanted and then didn't want to be bothered. So, off we go, traveling to clients' homes, sometimes more than 24 miles away so that they could continue to receive their assistance. The interesting and frustrating part was that we could be walking through the parking lot, returning from unsuccessful home contact attempts, and see the clients we were trying to locate drive right past us. We've already mailed out notification that time is running out for our agreed upon meeting and that we would be traveling to their homes, told them the dates and times, but to no avail.

I remember the cutest thing happened once. I ended up making the trip for nothing, but all I could think was, "Okay, ma'am, it's your choice." I wasn't perturbed about it, though, because a little child, maybe three years old, pulled back a sheer curtain from a tall window next to the door, looked up at me, and waved. He or she—I really couldn't tell, but the child had the most gorgeous thick blonde hair and yelled "Someone is at the door!" I waited and waited; eventually, the child ran along, but I still waited. After maybe five more minutes, I had to leave because this was the first of eight houses that I was scheduled to visit that day.

It always baffled me to see our clients drive by, just feet away from the building, but not caring enough about their assistance, supposedly their only source of income to stop in so that we could do our jobs. However, when their monthly payments were decreased because of their noncompliance some of them would call us everything from "amazing grace" to "how sweet the sound." It then became *our* crisis, not theirs, that they had lost some of their money. It was *our* fault that they had decided to keep driving instead of keeping an appointment or that other things were more important than stopping in and ensuring that the expected monthly amount would be there to support them and their families. I never could understand that.

Ok, so it was time to get ready for reviews, and I found that I had another form that needed a signature, so off I went to visit yet another household just to obtain signatures for a page or two. That day, I was furious about having to track down a particular client, a young mother who had compliance issues every month. This was the third time in two years that she had signed up to receive public assistance, and each time I had been responsible for her. She would either get a job or go to school and then, after a month or so, decide that it wasn't for her and sign up for assistance again. Needless to say, I was not a happy camper that day, nor did I find any humor in having to chase her down repeatedly so that she could continue to receive *her* free public assistance.

It was January, and it was cold out, and I was not smiling. I had already decided that this wasn't going to last and that I was tired of having to explain why some of my clients either hadn't found employment yet or had managed to botch the employment that we had helped them to secure. In my mind, I wanted to answer, "Why." I'll tell you why: because they've figured out that it's easier not to work, plus there are more perks for not working: that's why!" I would have probably been fired, but, at that point, I cared about as much as the young mother I was trying to track down. I had had it that day, I tell you!

I was already starving because lunch had to wait until I completed this task, and, when I arrived at her apartment building and found her unit, my hunger was even greater because whatever she was cooking smelled amazing. I knocked on her door, and she yelled, "Who is it?" in a tone that wasn't very welcoming, but I said my name and waited, and waited until she finally decided to come to the door. Because it was the dead of winter, I didn't just hold her screen door open while she signed the paperwork but decided to step inside. All of the sudden this little guy, who looked to be about two years of age, came running into the kitchen from the hallway, naked as a jaybird, male appendage and all, as happy as he could be. It was January, the January that's in the winter! His exposure to the cold didn't bother his mother, and she made no attempt to help me raise my bottom lip back up to my top lip. Eventually, I was able to blurt out, "He'll catch pneumonia!" The situation didn't phase her one bit; she signed the paperwork, he continued to play, and I left still stunned at what I'd just witnessed.

On the way back to the office, I thought that I would hate for my child to be sick because it would make me feel sick too, but then my mind started doing its "that would make a good research topic" thing that I couldn't seem to stop. I thought that, if her kid did get sick, she wouldn't have to worry about calling her employer to request the time off to take him to the doctor because she doesn't work. She wouldn't have to worry about finding the funds to pay for the office visit because it's already covered. She wouldn't have to worry about juggling a schedule to accommodate the appointment time because she was always available or could walk in whenever she chose. It didn't even matter how long the doctor's visit took because time was on her side.

Simply put, the things that people have to think about when they have sick children are far more complicated and stressful when they are employed. This is yet another argument that we, social workers out in the field, lose when trying to convince our clients to find jobs. For working parents, everything can suddenly revolve around a sick child, and they have to rearrange their lives to get through temporary crises. I was in our area's largest and best-known drug store one day and overheard two gentlemen. They greeted each other warmly, and one said that he heard that the other had been in the hospital. The other man acknowledged that he had indeed, but he seemed perturbed about the ambulance service that took him there. He grumbled, "They charged me $500 just to take me from"- I didn't catch the rest of what he said because I was paying the cashier, but I could imagine that the distance was nowhere near enough, in his mind, at least, to justify a bill for $500.

"Okay, so where are you going with all of this?" you ask. A couple of years ago, I knew a young couple, still in their teens, with two children, one around two years old and the other around six months. The parents had been fortunate enough to inherit their house, so they had no rent or mortgage to pay and even had two vehicles. To me, this was very impressive. Sadly, the young father had a chronic illness and had been receiving Social Security payments for much of his life. In addition, the older child had been born prematurely and barely survived and was

THERESA DIITI

also receiving Social Security payments—or his mother was, I should say—to cover expenses related to complications at birth.

The mother was also receiving public assistance for the youngest child amounting to more than $250 per month. I'm not sure whether the children, in addition, were receiving Social Security payments because of their father's health condition, but I do know that, in the case of a parent's death, minor dependents receive social security payouts. In addition, the family received food stamps, which and at that time, amounted to $632 per month for a family of four as well as food through the Women's, Infants, and Children (WIC) program .[1] The mother would occasionally secure employment, but her jobs usually lasted only a month or so. She was so intelligent and so gifted when it came to maintaining her household and income to support it that I often told her that she could work in Washington. She had such a quick mind when it came to making things work; it was truly amazing! (I deal with some of these issues also in the chapters titled "Strategies" and "CEO's and Millionaires Could Learn a Thing or Two.")

One day, her boyfriend, the children's father, became very ill and had to go to the hospital. The problem was, there was no gasoline in either vehicle, so the young lady made the decision to call an ambulance. "So!" you may be thinking, "she called for an ambulance…and?" Well here's the deal. At that time, one adult on disability would receive up to $733 per month in disability benefits,[2] and a child under the age of five received $650 per month in Supplemental Security Income (SSI) benefits[3]. Their household should have had at least $1,383 in monthly cash assistance without having to work for it. This figure does not include the other forms of assistance that they received, such as subsidized utilities. And remember: they paid no rent or mortgage to boot.

So what's the point? Here comes the "hail that ambulance" part! WHY WAS THERE NO GASOLINE IN EITHER VEHICLE? Why did the young lady decide to call an ambulance to get her boyfriend to the hospital? We were providing the cash assistance, but we were not mandating that they attend budgeting classes, though we offered and made such classes available at the time. We gave our clients what they wanted, but we really didn't impose any significant consequences if they didn't even try to make the assistance temporary and not a career. Thus, we were handing out lump sums of money–in their case, more than $1,550 on the first through the third of every month–but it's gone when it's needed the most. And where does the money come from to supply the free cash assistance that deters those who receive it from working? It comes–FROM A PORTION OF THE MONEY THAT IS EARNED BY THOSE WHO *ARE* WORKING!

Remember the gentleman at the drug store who had to pay $500 for an ambulance to take him to the hospital? Well, after hearing about the young lady's decision to call an ambulance because she had no gasoline, my *research mind* kicked in once again, and I phoned the ambulance service in our area. It took a couple of tries, but, eventually, I was able to connect with someone who had the numbers that I was looking for. "How many times has the service transported people to the hospital over the year?" I asked. "Two hundred and seventeen," he said. Given the size of the figure, I assumed that he had thought I meant annually. "Well," I replied, "217 calls a year isn't bad." "No", he explained, "that number is since January 1."

Our conversation was on January 15-the year happened to be 2014-so only a couple of weeks had yet passed. If each call was $500, how many of these emergency calls were paid for with cash, or, for seniors, through Medicare? And, if we're looking at low-income families that receive Medicaid, does coverage include all of the ambulance services needed? How do emergency medical services (EMS) make their money; who picks up the tab? (Further research is needed to quantitatively or qualitatively prove... and go from there graduate students, you-are-welcome.)

CHAPTER 8

Not Working for the Children

What does "not working for the children" have to do with being punished for working? When I worked with high-risk teens, I noticed that there were several common threads connecting them. When I say high-risk, I mean teens who had either already dropped out of school, were involved in the juvenile court system, were already parents or currently pregnant, or were receiving monetary or food assistance from the state. During my first meeting with them, almost every time, I learned that they were being raised in low-income households, as their parents and their parents' parents had been.

The field that I chose for graduate study (rehabilitation counseling) qualified me to work in several areas of human and social services. Each area provided me with valuable tools that I could use no matter where I was employed. When I was new to the field and attending agency meetings (which included wonderful lunches, by the way), I learned that prevention programs are the way to go when it comes to young people. Looking back now, I can't help but wonder whether these programs lived up to the expectations for them when they were implemented. I still believe, though, early prevention is a key consideration in at least some of the programs currently in place.

I had the opportunities to work with elementary, high school, and college-age students, and I remember to this day some of the situations that I encountered. In conversations with teachers and other school personnel during campus visits, I learned that some pretty unsettling things were going on, even with the early prevention programs in place.

A few years ago, one teacher asked me, "How can I perform my duties as an educator when I have to deal with a twelve-year-old girl who uses my classroom for naptime? She sleeps in my class because she was up with her infant all night long. And, since when do our job descriptions include having to be on guard because a student might freak out because of something going on, or not going on, at home?" I can't even begin to imagine what some teachers have to deal with just trying to perform their duties every day. What I *do* remember is that, when I got in trouble at school, I also go in trouble at home just because *the teacher sent a note home.* The teachers were the adults, and that's just how it was.

In addition to speaking with the teachers and the other school personnel, I engaged with parents because my job at that time involved serving as a liaison for at-risk students. Some of these parents expressed frustration, sharing with me that they couldn't discipline their kids out of concern that the state would take them away. Other parents, though, were cut from the same cloth as our parents *back in the day*, and they would gladly dial Child Protective Services before the butt-whooping commenced so that the caseworkers could arrive just as it was ending.

I started to learn early on that some things happen to us in order to prepare us for future situations. Back in the mid-eighties, I watched a young lady who lived across the street from me deteriorate because of her drug of choice. She was wildly in love with this substance and would boast about smoking it, all the while growing skinnier and skinnier. Fortunately, she didn't have any children.

While I was completing my internship at a halfway house, I was assigned to meet with various clients weekly for an hour so that I could practice reading, interpreting, and writing case notes. There were not many folks of color working at the halfway house—now that I think about it, I was the only one. Most of the residents had been referred to the facility by the court system, and they had no choice other than to be there for as many months as the courts deemed necessary.

When one woman in particular arrived, we immediately locked eyes, being of the same hue. She seemed relieved to see me. She said that she was scared to be 125 miles away from home and, worse, had temporarily lost custody of her children.

Over time, she had become increasingly distraught because it seemed that some of the other women there—not all, but some did not really accept her. Now, she was ready to throw up her hands and run away from the facility and go back to what she had grown accustomed to doing, which was living with her addiction.

I remember that we were sitting across from each other, almost knee to knee. She had been crying every day since arriving. During our meeting, she reached out, grabbed my hands, and rested her forehead on them, half-whispering, "I'm ready to give it up. I can't do this! I need to get back out there, and it's so painful because, when I'm out there, all I want to do is use. I don't even want to be with my kids when I'm off and running. I only want that drug, and I'm ready to give up everything to get back to it!" My heart ached for her because, once it was discovered that she had returned to the area, she would almost certainly be turned over to the Department of Corrections. We talked about the situation and she knew that she would lose her children permanently if she couldn't find family members to take care of them. Still holding my hand she whispered, "I don't know what will happen to them." She had already made arrangements for someone to pick her up, and in a few hours, she left. Every time I watch *Holiday Heart*[1], or *I Smile Back*[2], I think about her and the woman who lived across the street from me. This neighbor got thinner and thinner each time I saw her yet bragged about how wonderful this new drug was that she couldn't get enough of.

On one occasion, I was called to a school because a student kept attacking her teacher. I met with the young lady to assess the situation. Of course, according to the student, the teacher was always responsible for provoking these attacks. "She doesn't like me and she picks on me," the girl claimed. Little did I know that this emergency meeting would be the first of five concerning this girl. I met with the teacher, the school counselor, the principal, and, in the final session, the mother. I learned during the meeting that, because the school had been unsuccessful in persuading the mother to come to the school in the past, the next step would be for school personnel to contact Child Protective Services—which they eventually had to do. They had hoped that, by involving someone from an outside agency, namely me, they could at least let the troubled girl know that they were not kidding around.

After meeting with the school personnel, I had a little more insight into the child as well as her siblings. The next step was for me to meet with the mother at the family home. When I arrived, as usual, no one was there, or at least no one came to the door. The attacks on the teacher continued, so the school scheduled another meeting with the student and her mother. The woman probably received an invitation that she could not refuse—at least; this seemed to be why she arrived at a point when the meeting was almost over. In addition, her attire, strong smell of cigarettes, and bloodshot eyes suggested that she had come to the school straight from the club.

Once the school personnel started asking questions, the mother stormed out, apparently offended, leaving the student to fend for herself. For the first time, we saw the girl break down in tears, and she told us what had really been going on. We learned that she was so hot-tempered because, instead of being at home and in bed at night, she and one of her siblings were out in the street performing favors in exchange for money so that their mother "could buy cigarettes and other things." As I said, CPS had to be called after that disclosure, and I never heard any more about the case.

Years ago, I had the pleasure of being invited to a community empowerment luncheon where I met some movers and shakers. We mingled and enjoyed wonderful food; it was a good time, and we also learned a few things. A school administrator told a story at a break-out session that I will never forget about dealing with a young man who was so disruptive that he spent more time in the administrator's office than in the classroom. The student didn't have much of an explanation for his anger, so the administrator asked him what he did at home to deal with it. The teen replied that he went to his room and played video games so that he could "practice killing." I still get chills just thinking about it.

At the time, I wondered whether the teen was on medication and, if so, what would happen if he quit taking it when he reached adulthood. As the school administrator continued talking, I found myself thinking about this student just sitting in his room with so much anger that his only relief was pretending to kill people. I wondered what was really bothering this kid–issues at home, bullying, or even food insecurity?

There used to be a radio commercial on all the time about the things that kids do because they're hungry. One ad that particularly touched my heart, from an organization called Feeding America, was titled "I am Child Hunger in America." In it, a young girl voices the thoughts of various children, for instance, "I am a thirteen-year-old boy who gets into fights at school just because I'm hungry." The ad received criticism for its use of artificial intelligence (AI) but it struck a chord with me because of the school administrator's story about the angry young man. I suggest reading some of my Quora writings—such as "Why Do People Sell Their Food Stamps for Half the Amount They're Worth?" which you can find at the end of this book to get a clearer understanding of why low-income kids may go hungry even though their families receive food stamps. I do love organizations like Feeding America, especially when the public service announcements show children actually helping out at the food banks and pantries; this, in my opinion, sends a valuable message about children taking part and being active in their communities.

The fact is that, except when it comes to seniors and the homeless, I have a hard time wrapping my head around the issue of hunger in this country. I realize that people all over the world, including in the United States, still go hungry, but our food stamp programs, in this area anyway, started paying out double the usual amount in monthly food stamp benefits in March of 2020 and kept up the extra payments for more than a year. A friend invited me to her house recently and showed me three freezers full of food. With a smile, she said, "That's what all of those extra food stamps paid for."

I worked with a church a few years ago. The people there sent a mother and her twelve-year-old son to me who had just arrived in the area and needed a referral for a two-day stay at a local motel. She had driven most of the night, and the boy was angry at having to leave their home in another state. The mother explained that they had done so for safety reasons. When they arrived at the church, her car was almost out of gas. The boy went to play a video game in the common area for keeping children entertained while we met with their mothers about providing services.

I had completed the assessment and was preparing to print out the referral when the mother informed her son that he needed to end the game because it was time to go. This news seemed to anger him all over again, and, as they passed through our employee kitchen area, he punched his mother in the chest so hard that I was surprised he didn't crack a bone. His mother wasn't having any of it though, she grabbing him by the collar and slammed his back into the refrigerator. I applauded her because, had she crumbled and done nothing, her son could have gone from bad to worse and continued to attack and disrespect her. A friend once lamented to me that so many mothers have to raise their sons without fathers these days, pointing out that some boys try to intimidate their mothers; having watched their mothers suffer abuse, they think that they can dominate them by getting physical and "bringing it" or "stepping up" to their mothers.

For the job that I mentioned in "Plates as Big as States," my duties included conducting wellness checks. Once, I visited a facility at which two women were staying while they waited for their housing to become available. I enjoyed talking to them, but they were constantly at odds. Both were around forty, one being from a rural area and the other from a small urban area.

At some point, our discussion turned to foster homes, in which, it turned out, both had been raised. Unfortunately, this discussion became a sore spot for them for the next two weeks. The trouble started when the woman from the country expressed gratitude for some of her foster homes, asserting that living in them had kept her life from turning out a lot worse than it did.

The other woman responded with a terrifying fit of rage; I half expected to see knives and plates flying across the room since she was washing dishes at the time. She barked, "Well there's nothing I can say I was grateful for in any of the foster homes I lived in! All any of them did was help me survive when I was in prison. I couldn't even sleep at night wondering if it would be the foster fathers or their sons who would rape me this time!"

She went on to say that, no matter how much she would plead with the social workers to move her or try to tell them what was going on, nothing would ever change, so she kept running away from one foster home after another. She said that her clothes had always been dirty and too small and that, though she knew that the foster parents were getting money from the state for taking care of her, she never saw any of it. Before stepping outside to smoke a cigarette and calm down, she asserted that, when she was a young mother, she had done everything in her power to make sure that her children never ended up in foster care. Listening to her made me think that, in her case, foster homes and the system responsible for them had definitely failed.

When I returned the following week, the women still were not speaking, and, by the next week, one of them had been moved to another part of the facility. Both of the women were receiving disability payments–for what, I wasn't sure–and, as I mentioned, waiting to move into income-based apartments, which they did before the end of that month.

One summer, I worked with a sixteen-year-old girl who had just found out that she was pregnant with her first child. I discuss her story some more in "Hail that Ambulance." She was the funniest girl I ever worked with and smart as a whip. She could move and maneuver things in her life with such precision that she could teach a CEO or millionaire a thing or two. The young lady had had a hard upbringing. At a very young age, she had lost her mother, a well-known "street lady" who did whatever she had to in order to survive the violence around her and feed her addiction to drugs. She shared many stories with me about how hard she had it. Because of her difficult upbringing, she was very mature for her age. She described days passing without seeing her mother or finding her too "out of it" to make any sense, so she had pretty much raised herself.

This young woman would come to the workshop almost daily to use the computers and have a snack. When teens first started coming to the workshop, we entered them into our system so that they could receive the free services from the state that we provided. To do this, we needed proof of citizenship on some sort of identification such as a drivers' license. Once, I asked her why she only had a state I.D. rather than a drivers' license, since I saw her driving every day, and she replied, "I have too many tickets to get a drivers' license." Because she was so funny, I thought that she was just joking, but she went on to explain, "No, I've never had a license, but that doesn't stop me from driving, and it doesn't stop me from getting tickets, either, because sometimes I need to go somewhere (think Madea). She also said that her credit was shot and, when I asked her how that was possible for someone so young, she said that her mother had put things in her name and not paid the bills. I thought, "This poor kid!" Some people, including family members, do things that end up *not working for the children*.

CHAPTER 9

One Way or Another

My only argument with my best friend happened years ago. I was sitting at her kitchen table, pouting as usual about how I work my hind end off but still end up running out of cash. I was also irritated because I didn't want to go to work that day and going would cut our visit short. We always had such a good time, and she was the only person who actually got me. My friend was a stay-at-home mom, a long-time recipient of public aid–in her case, rightfully so, because she had a special needs child. She always had money, and I just couldn't figure out how. Well, I guess if I did the math, it would have made more sense. I mean, the rent for her three-bedroom house was next to nothing because it was based on her income which was zero, and she didn't have to pay for groceries. She just had to be cautious about her utility usage because, back then, there were no programs to subsidize utilities for low-income families.

What prompted the argument was a discussion of how some folks abuse public assistance. Maybe it was the funky mood that I was in, but her response when I asked her about what people would do if public aid ever stopped set me off. She said, "We'll just find another way to get it…one way or another." I didn't know why, but I started seeing weird colors and hearing a piercing sound like in the movie *Carrie* when the title character starts slamming doors shut and killing people. I'm sure my eyes looked just like Carrie's too. Little did I know that the words my friend spoke way back in the mid-1980s would prove to be prophetic.

Anyway, once I realized that I was, indeed, still on this planet, I barked at her, "How is it that you always have money but you don't work?" She replied, in the soothing tone that she was known for, and because she knew that she struck a nerve, "I have to make my money stretch because I only get paid once a month. I don't have a choice." Her words, "get paid," struck me. *What was she "getting paid" for?* I thought.

Years have passed since that conversation. I now understand that my friend was being paid to care for her two children, one, as mentioned, with special needs. She showed me a thing or two, though. She was an excellent money manager, and she went on to purchase two houses by saving what she could of her public assistance money, renting one out for additional income. Moving to the current day, I was informed that a recent emergency rental assistance program, in response to the COVID-19 pandemic, paid rent for qualifying applicants. Because of this program, a young woman that I know was able to save the money she would have used to pay rent, and instead, apply it toward a down payment on a house. In the meantime, I have watched my rent increase by $250 within two years' time. She shared that she takes home approximately $1100 in pay every two weeks but was still approved for, and took advantage of, this emergency rent program—one way or another.

After what seems like forever working in the field of public assistance, I have seen low-income clients use all kinds of methods to meet their needs. Some of the methods are so ingenious that I've asked myself if I'm just plain stupid or what? *Why can't I think of things like that?* "One way or another", as my friend said. In the chapter titled *Strategies*, I show the amount of ingenuity it takes to work the programs ("the system") to one's advantage, and one of my first experiences early on in my career is another example. Back in the nineties, many of my clients had to report to me for referrals for services that they needed, especially those preparing to take the "next step" when beginning to apply for disability benefits.

It takes time to learn when a worker is new to a field. My first and most painful experience, though not my last, occurred when I worked with a mother and daughter duo who were having fun with me—as I'll explain in a moment. I had just started in human and social services, and those who knew me were saying, "That ain't gonna last!" On this particular occasion, the drama started in the waiting room with wailing, raised voices, stomping, and things knocked to the floor. A woman in her twenties was having the kind of temper tantrum that I had only seen in toddlers. I was beyond nervous, but I had a job to do, so I ushered the woman, who was accompanied by her mother, into my office. I had no idea that I would still remember them thirty-two years later, but writing this book brought them back front and center.

The two of them had me busier than any other clients I would encounter in my career. I was jotting down notes, picking up papers and magazines off of the floor, and running to the door to keep the daughter from going back out into the hallway. They were visiting me to obtain a crisis referral to a small rural health agency, like so many others beginning the process of applying for disability. During this entire "crisis" encounter, the mother was laughing at her daughters' behavior which naturally puzzled me. I thought, "What was she laughing at?" All the mother could say was, "She acts like this all of the time. That's why we're here. She needs something, whatever you can do." She went on, "She needs a crazy check because she's…crazy!"

That's all I can share about what the mother thought of her daughter's issues. She could get away with saying the "C-word", but I cannot. I completed the assessment and required paperwork and made the referral phone call to set up an appointment for the "next step." I showed them out and gave them my business card and was glad to get back to my office and close and lock the door. Thankfully, it was lunch time, I had made it through my first encounter, not yet realizing that it was the beginning of an increase in families seeking and obtaining approval for disability.

Now I'll explain what I meant when I said that they were "having fun with me." About six months later, I was in a local store, and overheard two women talking and laughing, and I recognized the voices, especially the laugh. I kept shopping, looking up on occasion. You know the look you exchange with someone when you recognize them and they recognize you but not sure from where? The lightbulb went off for all three of us at the same time, and all of our eyes opened wide. The young woman realized that it was "show time," and, once again, the performance started! She transformed from a perfectly normal, even-tempered young lady enjoying shopping with her mother to an out-of-control, childish, fit-throwing nincompoop.

The mother had a look of embarrassment on her face, and I'm sure I had a look that was half hurt and half flabbergasted realizing that I had been duped. The image instantly formed in my mind of the mother saying on the drive to my office that day, "Okay, we're almost there. Now I want you to go in and act a plumb fool! I want you to clown as if your life depended on it!" How foolish I felt learning that the daughter's mental problems had all been a game, an act, and they were partners in crime all the while. My only satisfaction from seeing them was to give them a look making it clear that I was disgusted with them and they should be ashamed of themselves.

The story didn't end there, though. Years later, even after I started working for another agency that provided services for the homeless, almost on a daily basis, I kept hearing, "I'm on disability." I started to grow concerned. Even more alarming, on the occasions that I had to verify clients' income, if they had any, a growing number of children in the household were either already on disability, or were trying to start receiving disability. It seemed that receiving disability was becoming the main source of income in more and more households, and I continued to have this perception throughout my career.

While working in a somewhat different occupation, one that I thought I wouldn't have to deal with these issues, I'd look out over the parking lot while I waited for clients to arrive for their appointments, and I'd see things that just didn't make sense. There was a pep in their step after getting out of their vehicles like the dance moves of Fred Astaire. There were folks jumping so high off the beds of their pick-up trucks that pole vaulters would be green with envy—a bit of an exaggeration, of course, but I have seen wondrous feats right outside my office, especially when clients were coming to receive a benefit... *one way or another.*

Watching those in need walk to the door would also confused me, and I could only conclude that the entry to the building was cursed. Once, I watched a client I knew lean through a car window for a man to light her cigarette. She held a cervical collar for her neck in her other hand as she laughed and socialized with the man in the car. Somehow, though, after walking through the entryway into the building, her neck grew so stiff that she could barely move it, and—you guessed it—she donned the cervical collar and became a very different sight from the woman I had just seen in the parking lot.

On another occasion, I worked with a woman so clever that I found myself shaking my head in awe when she told me her plans. I liked seeing her and her children walk through the door because the children were always so well-behaved. She explained that she wanted to be put on the waiting list to receive furnishings and household goods because she was getting closer to purchasing a house. She informed me that she was receiving disability, as were her teenage daughter and one of her young sons. She went on to say that she just received a letter informing her that a disability hearing has been scheduled for her youngest son (he may have been in kindergarten) and that she expected approval of his claim in the near future.

Smiling, she explained that, once he's approved, she would be able to put money down on a house because each person in her household would be receiving over $733 to $766 a month at the time of this writing. With at least $3,000 per month in disability income, I imagined the wonderful home she and her children would have. I asked her what the issues were with her children that they had to receive disability, noting how well-behaved they always were. "Oh you don't know my kids," she replied. "They don't know how to act when they're in school; they act out!"

My first thoughts were for the poor teachers since I had witnessed plenty of inappropriate behavior, sassy mouths, and nasty attitudes first-hand while working with the schools. Having been made such a fool of early on in my career, I was skeptical and started wondering whether she was giving her kids a pep-talk telling them how they needed to act so that their behaviors would be documented as indicating a disability. That is, she may have been encouraging her children to wreak havoc in their classrooms so that she could sign them up for programs that would provide funds that she could then use to buy a house. Particularly concerning to me was the fact that children are often put on medications to help with behavior issues as seen in disability cases, some then decide to take themselves off the medications once they come of age.

At the beginning of this book, I indicated that there would be instances where I would say, "More research is needed to examine, to conclude, to identify, to propose—and I can certainly imagine a few research projects that this chapter could inspire namely, the effects of coaching behaviors in children; the disability application process.

CHAPTER 10

Solid as Smoke

Have you ever stuck your hand through a puff of smoke? The smoke just sort of dissipates, doesn't it? One of the things that inspired *Punished for Working* was my recognition of patterns in the families that relied on public assistance programs for income rather than working. Some believed that the only *guaranteed* source of income available for them came, not from employment, but from programs run by the state and government. This was especially true in rural communities, where there tend to be few employment opportunities in the first place.

This belief seems especially common among individuals who have depended on assistance programs for many years and even more so among those whose families have been recipients of aid for generations. I was being paid to try to change negative perceptions about working, but I found that I was in a constant battle with no chance of winning. Usually, by the time my clients were fed up with me for pushing them out of their comfort zones, it was safer to just retreat and *leave things alone* which was the complete opposite of what I was supposed to do. I heard more than once that folks came to the area where I worked because our agency offered particularly large public assistance pay-outs and not because of the job opportunities. Other states were paying out even more than mine, and some of my clients told me of their plans to move to one of them.

One woman I was working with told me that she and her kids were moving to a northern state for this reason and because the waiting list for Section 8 housing was shorter there. I wondered whether she had even taken the time to consider that the cost of living might be higher, too, but some things are just not worth arguing about. I made the mistake once of asking a long-time resident whether he had ever thought about relocating for better opportunities such as employment, and his reaction was so extreme that it almost activated my fight or flight response.

The sad thing is that so many people out there are convinced that, because public assistance programs have always been there for them, they have no need to worry about these programs ever being discontinued. My colleagues and I would sometimes discuss the need for major restructuring or even elimination of some of the programs, because they result in dependence. In fact, some assistance programs have not only replaced working but even reward individuals for *not* working. In my opinion, they're hurting families more than helping them because they take away self-sufficiency. These kinds of programs gave some of the families that I worked with the false sense that their lives as beneficiaries were the best that they could hope for. Such beliefs obviously limit human potential–especially the potential to become independent through working and end reliance on systems that could one day dissipate like a puff of smoke.

The frustrating part of my work in this field, and the reason that I decided to change careers, was that, no matter where I suggested my clients apply for work, there was always an excuse, or ten excuses, why a particular job just wouldn't work for them. On a drive to the store one Saturday, within twenty minutes, I saw three establishments with "help wanted" signs taped to their windows or doors. When I mentioned this observation to some of my clients the following Monday, I heard, "Okay," but the looks on their faces suggested that I was just wasting my time telling them about these possible opportunities. One gentleman even said, "They don't hire felons!" My response was, "How do you know they don't hire felons?" He said, "Because it's always on the job application." During our next meeting, I asked, "So, what did they say after you turned in the application?" He said, "Nothing." Then I asked, "Did you even go in to fill out the application?" When he affirmed that he had, with my blood pressure rising, I said, "I'll bet you went in there will a bullhorn announcing that you're a felon; you probably even had on a tee-shirt with the word "felon" printed on it just to make sure that you wouldn't have to take a minimum-wage job. Having a job would cramp your style by putting an end to your sitting around and playing like a kid all day!" Sometimes, I just had to get feelings like this off of my chest or risk losing my sanity! That was indicator number 341 that it was time for me to find something else to do for a living.

There were, however, times when clients did indeed secure employment after following up on tips that I provided, though usually they would only stick with a job for a paycheck or two. Once more, work eventually reduced or put an end to the assistance they had been receiving. I would hear that childcare was too expensive to keep working–even when the state made childcare assistance programs available. I'd hear that the pay was too low or that the hours were too early or too late. A client even used "It was raining" as an excuse for not going to work one day. Others told me that they had quit working because "My rent went up" or "My food stamps got cut." There were so many excuses for not working that, eventually, I was too exhausted even to try to convince clients that they should still do so.

When I started writing this book, there were more people working than not working, but I thought, "What if, one day, there were more people *not* working than there are working?" Little did I know back then that a time would come when this would be the case, for now fewer people are working than there have been for a long time, and businesses are having a hard time finding employees. The stimulus money delivered as part of the government's Covid-19 response was a blessing for those who received it–or for me, at least–but it encouraged more people to be content with working less and relying on hand outs. In other words, this cash appeared to diminish the importance of independence gained from working since it showed those who had only received money in the form of paychecks how much easier and even more lucrative it can be to live on various forms of assistance.

The problem, then, occurs when benefits from the government are more appealing than the rewards of punching a time clock. As we're seeing now, all forms of assistance have potential downsides. The eviction bans that formed as part of the pandemic response, for example, seem to have done more harm than good for some families based on the number that appear to have nowhere to go once the bans are lifted.[1] We have failed some of these families with these "*rent pardons*," as I like to call them, because we were not educating the recipients of public assistance—and, where necessary, issuing dire warnings—in preparation for the cessation of benefits. Advertisements on television and radio as well as social media could have reminded families that the eviction moratorium was temporary even though the deadline was extended several times. Now that this policy has come to an end, news stories indicate that some families remain in jeopardy of losing their homes—so, what was it all for? Also, as a result of this policy, rent, has now risen to the point that it is difficult for some families to remain in their homes.

I found nothing more disheartening than meeting with clients who depended on us and us alone, for their wellbeing. When I asked my clients what they would do if the programs ever went away, most of them had never thought about it—again, because the programs have always been there for them while others replied that they would cross that bridge when they came to it.

A restructuring of current programs so as to give to able-bodied recipients the ultimatum either to meet us halfway In order to get their needs met will happen sooner rather than later, I suspect. Programs such as Habitat for Humanity come to mind when I think about mandating clients' participation in order to receive benefits, in this case, a new house resulting from the combined efforts of the construction workers, volunteers, and the people who will live in it. The new home owners have to put in the hours, or their houses won't be built! When eligibility requirements are strengthened, social service workers' caseloads decrease, and, with fewer repeat clients, we can work toward eliminating dependence on programs that may one day turn out to be only as solid as smoke.

CHAPTER 11

Strategies – CEOs and Millionaires Could Learn a Thing or Two

As mentioned, at one point in this project, I met with a publisher, who urged me to keep working on it since people like him had almost no knowledge of the inner workings of the public aid system and rarely knew anyone who received assistance. However, he said that he was aware that the system influences, and sometimes discourages, the desire to work. I appreciated the time that he spent listening to the ideas that have gone into *Punished for Working*, but I realized right away that he wasn't willing to wait a hundred years for me to finish it. I, on the other hand, have been in no hurry to wrap things up.

THERESA DIITI

Sometimes, I sit in absolute amazement when I think about the determination that propelled powerful people such as Edith Flagg, Daymond John, and Tyler Perry to the pinnacle of success. I'm sure that their journeys were not free of adversity; in fact, I'm almost positive that some of the challenges that they faced were responsible to some extent for their achievements. I wonder especially whether they relied on specific strategies to navigate their journeys. That said, I believe that we all have natural talents, something that we're born with, that we are sent here to do, and to which we are drawn. I don't personally know anyone who has pursued something that they did not find interesting and been able to stick with it for very long.

I remember being called every name in the book by a parent who phoned my office years ago because I was not encouraging her son to go into nursing as she had done. She didn't understand the responsibilities of my position–working with at-risk students, in part, because I had once been one nor, it turned out, did she know that her child was failing anatomy and physiology, a must-pass course for students hoping for a career in any medical field. This mother apparently knew nothing about the many meetings that I had had with the instructor for the course. She showed me the student's exam grades, all Fs, in her grade book and explained that he seemed unhappy and stressed in class, with no desire to be there and no interest in the subject. *Fs across the board does not a good medical practitioner make.*

I also knew, though, because of almost daily meetings with him, that this student had an amazingly gentle, kind, and caring nature, and he felt anguished about the situation, shedding tears over having to take a class that he hated. Sensing that medicine may not have been his calling, I told him about helping professions in which he might make better use of his natural gifts and talents. Introducing him to other aspects of the field so that he could remain in school was the strategy I chose to use because his days were numbered. This strategy was successful: he went on to graduate from a four-year university and then complete an accelerated master's program in social work. He probably ended up earning as much if not more than his mother ever dreamed he would as a nurse. Years later the mother apologized to me, with her son living a happy life–something that I have always felt should come first and foremost. While working in human and social services, I think the thing that wowed me the most was the expertise and strategies of the people we served. I received "an education" regarding the ways in which people played the system to get what they wanted. I was constantly amazed as I received this education at the *sheer genius* of some of my clients. They were better at my job than I was. With one young lady in particular, the only thing missing was a dry-erase board, she was so experienced that she could have diagrammed the strategies that she used to get by. She seemed quite proud of herself, teaching me how easy it was to make the rounds from one agency to another so that she could live for free. On occasion, she would give me a sideways glance as if to say, "Girl, you know how it's done. Quit playing!"

These folks' meticulous plans to get what they needed from the state simply blew me away! And here I am, going to work every day–just plain stupid of me, I guess. As they told me how it's done, I could envision them creating training manuals and programs for CEOs and millionaires that, if followed correctly, could help them far surpass their current levels of success. My clever clients taught me more about the *game* and how to play it than I ever could have figured out for myself. It occurred to me that, just as the wealthy know how to pass *the secrets* down from generation to generation, those who have mastered living on public assistance for years have been passing the torch in the form of strategies for dealing with agencies like mine—and why not? If it works, it works!

After being employed in the field for a couple of years, I started paying particular attention when I saw grandparents, parents, and their teens among my caseloads that were all from the same families. When I noticed a certain last name and asked whether a client was some kin to so-and-so, the answer was almost always "Yes." So, you might be thinking, "That's because usually the entire family is poor!" to which I say, "Yes, that's usually the case. However, I reiterate that I worked with the grandparents all the way down to the grandchildren, families that can be described as living in generational dependence. Perhaps the problem is that there are no services available that could end the generational dependence, or that all of the facets of the services that *are* out there, do not prepare clients for self-sufficiency effectively enough. Or perhaps there is simply no interest in even *hinting* at the thought of ending the public assistance relationship. The "hidden education" that I received taught me that getting off of one form of assistance or another usually wasn't the plan when people came to see me. The folks I met with did not appear to be interested in talking about anything other than getting what they had come for. When, by chance, I couldn't locate the funds to pay for what they wanted, they would ask about other programs or agencies, indicating that they were going from one agency to the next. The monies from funding sources are only available until they are used up. Programs come and go, funding can also be maxed out, especially when children reach the age at which the assistance is reduced or eliminated.[1]

In my Quora piece, "Do people live off welfare?" I tried to break down how to survive quite nicely on the limited income that the state provides. The strategies that low-income families use to make it from month to month are the same ones used in households that don't receive government support. These strategies involve identifying what needs to be paid in order to survive: members of the household require a roof over their heads (housing), electricity, water, heating, and air conditioning (utilities), nutrition (food), wellness (health-care), and child care (day-care and babysitting). These are the basics; some households may have other necessities, for example, a running and, hopefully, licensed and insured vehicle.

Whether or not they receive government support, then, the members of households develop strategies. Households that do receive support may use it to pay some or all of the rent (housing) depending on the income requirements. These considerations remind me of a sociology class that I took many years ago in which the professor described a constant but ever-changing, kaleidoscopic pattern of residents who live in inner cities, who move to more upscale neighborhoods, often in the suburbs, to enjoy a higher standard of living, and often with the help of programs such as Section 8 housing.

Then, as housing in these neighborhoods becomes scarce, some residents move back to the inner city. The pattern repeats over generations, driven by the desire to enjoy more amenities, greater security, and so on. The professor also said that, eventually, some family members may have to consider moving in with other families because of housing or economic crises. Reflecting on the end of the eviction moratorium, I wonder whether this merging of households will now become a trend.

Energy assistance programs subsidize utility payments. Usually, families that receive rental assistance or food stamps also qualify for other forms of assistance, including with utilities. Some of the families that I worked with qualified for nine months' worth of assistance from such programs, as much as $1,600 per year. One young lady told me, when it was time for her to renew her application that she had $13.10 to apply toward her bill. When I checked, I found that she indeed had exactly that amount remaining from her yearly utilities allotment. Her careful calculations in getting the most out of her assistance showed me the same kind of talent, skill, know-how, ingenuity, and timing that CEOs and millionaires display.

Turning now to food, for those who qualify for grocery assistance, obtaining enough food to eat is easier than it is for households that do not receive food assistance, such as SNAP benefits. Again, whether or not they receive government support, households develop strategies for making sure that everyone is fed. A grocery budget, sometimes a quite frugal one, is usually a must, with specific weekly, biweekly, and monthly purchases (as mentioned in "Plates as Big as States").

Moving on to healthcare, the Affordable Health Care Act has extended coverage to more Americans than ever before.[2] Earlier, those who worked full-time and brought in an income that put them over the poverty line, were reluctant to visit a doctor (as mentioned in "Hail that Ambulance!"). Even now, for those who do not receive some form of assistance or have health insurance, the expense of a visit to a walk-in clinic makes this choice an absolute last resort.

Years ago, while working my way through school, I had a job as a server along with the other gigs I had to make ends meet. Once, just after Christmas, a co-worker told me that she would be quitting the restaurant soon because business had decreased by half after the holiday, so we were making hardly anything. She said that she had two little girls, and that her husband's jobs were always iffy, so continuing to pay for daycare services without receiving much in tips was "killing us". She told me that she was paying $300 a week for the girls' daycare, and this was more than twenty years ago. At the time, I had never heard of such an outrage, because she was right: it didn't make sense for her to keep working.

Years later, I heard the same thing from those who came to my office for my agency's services. They would explain the cost of working, and I would have to agree. I was able to help them qualify for childcare at minimal or no cost. This type of childcare assistance was meant to enable parents to join the workforce or continue their education. Of course, I would hear excuses for not accepting the free childcare, and, again, sometimes, I would have to admit that my clients' reasoning was sound. I heard, "People have said bad things about that place"; "I went to school with the girl who runs it, and I don't want her taking care of my children"; "It's too far; how am I supposed to get my kids there?"; or even "I'm not interested in gas vouchers, either." Often, I showed them options for daycare, but the clients would find ways to decline.

When the government does not provide assistance with childcare, a household with children has a very real and substantial financial burden. So that the parents can make a living, one may stay home, because if both continue to work, the bulk of their income goes toward childcare. Of course, the pandemic has been changing the situation even as I have been writing.

Back in the day, other family members would step in to care for grandchildren, nieces, nephews and cousins. Back in the day, I'm sure, when possible, there were forms of compensation for this kind of childcare, but we never saw it. Now, parents can designate grandparents or other family members to care for their children in exchange for payments from the government.[3]

My clients who had learned the ins and outs of "getting over" taught me that it is mainly just a matter of making ends meet. They take care of what is due first and find out which agencies pay for whatever else they may need. They sign up immediately to receive rental assistance to have a place to live because the waiting lists are always long. Then, once their applications are approved, it's just a matter of being reevaluated every year to continue to receive the rental assistance. Next, they identify the agencies that subsidize power and heating bills and apply for health care and child care, if they are interested in the latter. Having met the needs, the family is good to go for a month, year, or even longer.

Another strategy is coordinating applications for services that need to be filed at various times throughout the year or, in some cases, less frequently. Once all of the pieces are in place, the family has only to keep the various appointments to ensure that everything gets paid for. The problem is this doesn't always happen. When a crisis hits and services are needed right away (like yesterday), those of us who administer them seem like the devil's spawn if we can't help. However, we are powerless because those who need the services don't always do what they were supposed to do, namely, keep their appointments. We become the punching bags, and we're supposed to take the punches with a smile. We end up being you got it!-*punished for working*. I'm sure that folks who work 50, 60, 70 hours a week would love to have a schedule that required them to leave the house for appointments only half a dozen or so times a year to ensure they will receive what they need.

So, I learned, as part of my hidden education, that, at least in our area, people can live well off of welfare by taking advantage of every available assistance program, managing their resources carefully, and making the most of opportunities such as free recreational activities. Keep in mind, this strategy requires living a very simple and frugal life, but it's possible-I saw it happen every day. For example, families that receive $259 a month from Temporary Assistance for Needy Families (TANF) can secure apartments through public housing or Section 8 vouchers. With food stamps and energy assistance, they are pretty much set for the month.

A family receives an apartment in public housing through the Housing Authority based on a percentage of its TANF allotment. So, if its subsidized rent is $59, $200 is left to live off of for the month. Some public assistance housing includes utilities, and some does not. Those who do have to pay their own utilities may be eligible for the aforementioned energy assistance programs. Thus, families that receive TANF payments are almost guaranteed approval for utility assistance, and TANF and SNAP (food stamps) go hand in hand, so there is no need to worry about money to purchase groceries. Personal items and things like cleaning supplies can be purchased with the remaining $200 on the EBT card. How much bleach, floor cleaner, furniture polish, and so on does a family need to purchase monthly? Dish-washing detergent and laundry detergent, I can see, but…

For recreation, families often have the option of taking the kids to the library where free movie and music rentals are available. Many cities and towns have free museums, parks, and recreation centers. In our area, residents can experience live music in the park (just bring food in a cooler). One of the classes that I taught is money management, in which the students calculate how to live on the monthly state assistance allotment. With $200 a month left on the card or $50 a week in-pocket for cab fare or to chip in for gasoline to go to the store, and with everything else already paid for, the family is pretty much set. I'm witness to the fact that people with the right strategies have lived and are living on government support, sometimes for generations.

I was completing a practicum at one of the homeless shelters in the area when I was introduced to a gentleman I'll call Jim. I had seen him around town from time to time but never paid him much attention. He was approximately 40 years old, and was usually smiling as if someone were talking to him. I would see him lying in the grass under trees or smoking and drinking coffee at one of the coffee shops in the area (people could smoke anywhere back then, even professors in classrooms). One day when I arrived to complete my hours, there he sat at the dinner table, eating with the rest of the group. Some were residents at the shelter and some were just there for the meal.

He reminded me a little of Sam Kinison because he was around the same size and had long wavy hair and wore a beret and a long trench coat like the comedian. His fingertips and fingernails were yellow from the tar in the many cigarettes that he smoked. That day, after he had finished eating, Jim went outside to smoke and sit under a tree enjoying the weather. A little later, he came back and sat in the living room area with a big grin on his face, again, as if someone were talking to him. He produced a book that he always seemed to carry with him from his backpack and began to read. I introduced myself at this point, but I was a little nervous because I wasn't quite sure about how to approach him. I found myself talking to him very cautiously, almost as if he were a child, because I didn't know how much he could comprehend. My caution made him grin even wider because, as I soon found out, I was making a fool of myself. He was polite; he spoke softly and used few words. I got the feeling that he really didn't want to be bothered.

I moved on to greet the other people who were socializing after eating and then stopped in to visit with one of the counselors on staff. The counselor observed, "So, you met Jim." I acknowledged that I had and asked what his story was. The counselor explained that Jim was a genius and asked whether I had noticed what he was reading. When I replied that I had not, he said that he was probably immersed in some sort of classic in German or one of the two other foreign languages that he spoke. He explained that Jim could also solve any math problem that someone put in front of him. I remembered then that big grin on his face while I was talking to him and realized that it was a nice way of calling me an idiot. The counselor explained that Jim wanted nothing to do with rules or responsibilities and mainly lived outside to avoid having to pay rent, except during the winter months when he lived at the shelter. He also confirmed what I had observed, that Jim enjoyed sleeping in the grass and looking up at the trees, he visited the library almost every day, and he loved his cigarettes and his own company.

Over my years working in social services, I ran across many people who felt the same way. Some were homeless by choice, having no interest in paying bills or having to be somewhere at a certain time, such as having a job. I sometimes feel a little guilty because, in a way, we helped to make this nomadic lifestyle easy to sustain. The years and the experiences that came along with them helped me to realize that some people find it easy to accept circumstances for which, in my mind, there is neither rhyme nor reason. At the same time, clients have proved to me repeatedly their capacity to survive for years practicing their own methods, some of which are pure genius.

CHAPTER 12

Stamp 'Em Through, Get Paid, and Shut Up!

We seem to go through several stages of molding ourselves to fit our careers. As we move toward the retirement stage, we usually change at least a little (and probably a lot); we're different from the people who we were when we started in our fields. Along the way, we have gathered the tools that we needed to be successful, and we have learned the tricks to preforming our duties. When it comes to our passions, the motivation for doing what we do often originates in a very personal place.

An individual's career path may reveal itself early. Children who display nurturing characteristics, for instance, may be well-suited to work as caregivers, while those who like making sandcastles may have the interest and aptitude to work as engineers or inventors, and those who make costumes out of bath towels and run around in the front yard like they've lost their minds (my favorite kind of youngster) may be cut out for work in the entertainment industry. The environment may also influence children's thinking about life as an adult, such as growing up in a household with a mother who is a doctor or a father who is a policeman. When I was a child, I had the impression that my family didn't really care what I did as long as I worked and would not be depending on them to take care of me once I was old enough to take care of myself.

I remember once, while employed in social services, walking down the hall to my cubicle and scanning the faces of my coworkers as I passed them. The younger ones, I noticed, who were just getting started, were just happy to receive their paychecks and energetically ran to their cars to go out and *save the world*. We all felt this passion right after graduating as the next generation of workers who would dedicate our lives to making the world a better place. We couldn't think about or even see anything else, and we were so precarious financially, because of our student loans that we had no choice other than to be at that job (oh yes, I remember it well).

Those who had been working in the field for less than a decade, though, were always worried about meeting deadlines and getting the results that would lead to the renewal of their grants and security of their jobs. They were meticulous, capable of spotting an error in a spreadsheet from across the room. They also drove the newest and the fanciest vehicles, by the way.

The seasoned workers, those with decades or more of service behind them, on the other hand, were the ones who had really "made it," in my opinion. They had raised their kids and were helping with the grandkids; they had paid off their houses and had bank accounts with balances that would amaze the younger workers; and they were just waiting for their last day of work so that they could enjoy retirement. These old-timers were the ones I envied because they were relaxed, having the attitude that "A hundred years from now, who's going to know about it anyhow?" They were also the workers who seemed to chuckle when we acted like our world was coming to an end because our clients didn't achieve the outcomes for which we had been hoping.

These older workers were wonderfully patient and would let us waste their time sitting in their cubicles and offices just to vent. When we were done complaining and beating ourselves up even though we had done everything we could, they would lean forward and say in a low voice, "They came to get what they wanted and needed. Just s*tamp 'em through, get paid, and shut up!*" They knew from years of experience that we couldn't save all of those who came to us because some of them might not want to be saved. They knew all about the excitement of breaking through and reaching a client but also those breakthroughs don't happen every time. They also knew that, if they didn't take care of themselves, they would be of no use to anyone else, so they didn't punish themselves when things didn't work out.

Just as the years had seasoned them like an impeccably prepared porterhouse steak, the veteran social workers I encountered appeared to accept the fact that, just as one case closed two more would open. They balanced their lives, working until quitting time ("all pencils down") and then going home without looking back. That balance was the ticket, the secret to long-term paychecks and what really mattered. Doing their best was all that they could do, and they were no longer willing to be caught up in the madness that sometimes came with the territory in which we worked.

It wasn't a matter of not caring but rather the realization that the parade of the needy would never end. There will always be an ample supply of repeat clients and families and those who come to us as the first resort instead of the last. After so long, working to survive, working to provide, working to secure, working to have, and working to save–these were the pleasant thoughts that helped us get through the day

CHAPTER 13

Previous answers from Theresa Diiti published on Quora

Questions are exactly as they appear on Quora. (How it all started, before the editing, before the suggestions and recommendations, before the frustrations, and before pulling all of my hair out by the roots).

Effects: Generational dependence on public assistance programs.

THERESA DIITI

Are people who receive food stamps at all ashamed of it?

Answered May 22, 2016, (revised).

Well, it depends. I have a dear friend who drives eighteen miles when she purchases groceries with food stamps. Her embarrassment however comes from supporting her boyfriend of over 25 years. Because he doesn't want to work, she had no choice other than to accept the fact that he signed up for food stamps as a means of contributing to the household. This happens all the time, in more households than you can shake a stick at, when everyone who can work is choosing to opt out of working.

That said, there are others who seem to proudly whip their EBT cards out. Almost fine dining compared to my choices of, "Will it be bologna, rice, and eggs, or bacon rice and eggs tonight?" Don't get me wrong, I could fine dine too, but my paychecks go toward rent, lights, (none of which are at a discounted rate, or free for that matter). The money we're paid for working is just not enough sometimes. If wages go up, so does everything else, so we're chasing and chasing and not catching anything-including a break!

When I'm working with clients who feel that working is a losing battle, and I'm trying to convince them that it's not, by the time they get done telling me what they will lose if they worked, I usually end up looking pretty stupid.

What online grocery/food delivery services accept EBT cards/food stamps?

Answered May 29, 2016, (revised).

To my surprise, there is a pizza chain that has posted on its door that they accept EBT cards. When discussing this with a friend, who has food stamps, she advised that yes, as long as the food is NOT cooked it could be purchased with EBT cards. She went on to advise that even some restaurants, as long as the order is PAID FOR via EBT BEFORE the food has been cooked, accept this form of payment.

Why is SNAP considered to be a handout when you lose your job and apply for food benefits?

Answered June 5, 2016, (revised).

For those who have worked and paid in, of course they should be able to apply for and receive food stamps. But that's just it; there are numerous amounts of individuals/families who have not worked, sometimes ever! I was saddened when I realized that I was assisting folks who were in their 30's and have never held employment. One young lady didn't even know how to complete a job application. To be able to survive and not have to work to do it, now that's entrepreneurism!

If you've worked or are working and have paid in, I feel it's your right to apply for benefits. If you're approved to receive them, then your income, or the lack thereof, has met the state requirement guidelines that say you should have food benefits. You have paid your tax dollars to help feed yourself, your family, and other families as well.

How do I transfer SNAP benefits to another state if I move to another state but remain resident in the first?

Answered June 12, 2016, (revised).

I would call the Food Stamp office in your future state/county to find out their application process, (if you can reach someone that is, in our state, if you don't go in in person, the only other option is the automated system). Also, ask the approximate wait time for your food stamp case to be activated in the new state.

If you coordinate both your notification times, you hopefully won't have to wait too long between the time you requested your initial case to be closed, and your new case to be opened for the next allotment of benefits. Our wait time has sometimes taken 2 months due to missing information or inaccurate information. If there is an emergency situation like a fire, or food loss due to a flood, your case can sometimes be pushed through a little faster.

What are some possible alternatives to America's welfare system?

Answered June 12, 2016

If our economy continues to grow, and with jobs on the rebound, we will eventually have to start holding long-term or generational welfare recipients accountable for receiving it. The job market is already improving significantly, so it's becoming easier to secure employment for those who want to do so. For individuals who are avoiding job searching or working, a deterrent is the first thing that comes to mind when trying to discourage welfare dependence.

Signing up for, and receiving welfare assistance may need to return to the level of difficulty it once was back in the 60's and 70's. Back then, signing up for welfare often times weren't worth the bother because too much was required in order to start receiving it or to keep it.

Programs such as **subsidized employment**, (which are grant-funded), pay the employee's hourly wage for a short period of time. They, in my opinion, have proven to be successful for the most part. Business owners take advantage of the "free labor" for the time allotted, while the potential employee obtains job skills while being paid. When successful, the training and new job skills got some TANF recipients back into the workforce. Sometimes people just need to start somewhere.

Training Centers, (and I'm a strong advocate for them), for individuals who did not complete high school. **Job Corps** rates number 1 in my book because it lets young adults get back in the game, (if they really want to succeed that is). It depends on who you talk to, but if education and training is truly desired, Job Corps is the closest thing to attending college or a university that I've found. It incorporates hands-on training along with getting an education.

The only negative things I have heard about this wonderful organization came from young people who did not like structure or discipline. Other side of the coin, when I worked with inmates, if given the choice and they had it to do all over again, they would have jumped at the chance to attend Job Corps and learn a trade and work, over their current circumstances.

Along with Job Corps, I feel deeply that **apprenticeship programs** will return in full force and will help individuals acquire specialized skills that bring higher pay alleviating long-term dependence on welfare programs. Apprenticeship training is attractive because a good majority of our service population is simply not interested in continued education. Hands-on job preparation does not appear to require the whole, "school thing" that some of our younger clients chose to leave. The problem is however, some of your young program participants may only be reading at a fourth or fifth grade level, something they didn't take into consideration prior to making the decision to drop out of school, and our teachers can only do so much.

Apprenticeship programs do require reading, writing, math, spelling, reasoning, decision making, etc., but we work with a measurable amount of individuals who do not have a high school education. In a couple of cases, I've worked adults who do not know how to complete job applications, (program dependency, and completing job applications or securing employment, are almost like oil and water sometimes).

General assistance, (GA) was another program from way back, but as I remember, it required participation or no benefits-period! Those who received GA were required to sign up for any and every other program first, and once denied from all the other programs, saved for food stamps, they could then apply for GA. This program required the participant to report to a work site and complete hours first. After the required hours were completed, then, they received payment or vouchers or both, but not before. (General Assistance used to issue vouchers for personal or non-food items in addition to the cash benefit).

If money is going to continue to be poured into welfare programs, or if we are starting to look at ways to replace said programs, I feel that it would be in our best interest to focus on ways that provide training or retraining. As a means of making sure that the cash portion of the TANF benefit is not being misspent, half of it could be issued as a stipend or voucher that could be used to assist with utility payments or other venders used by the family. Assistance for utilities could be restructured in a way so that vouchers could be used in place of government or state disbursements to energy assistance programs and then dispersed again to the utility companies. The difference being, with stipends and vouchers, work hours would have to be completed in order to receive them. This allotment is still assistance, but it's half of the cash portion of TANF which is sometimes misspent or used for purchases that do not benefit the family.

A little off task but I've learned from working in the field not to use the word "volunteer" because it would result in an argument that I could never win. The most difficult task was to explain to the "volunteer" that hours have to be completed in order to receive the assistance. If I had a dollar for every time I heard, "I'm not volunteering anywhere!" I would have been long retired by now.

As the argument gets underway, I usually interject, "You are not volunteering, you are receiving free money from the government and state, you are required to complete the hours in order to continue to receive your free money." It never ended well but that's because assistance, in almost any form, has come to be expected without having to do anything for it.

Lastly, **day-workers,** and wish they were everywhere. This, in my opinion, could significantly reduce the number of assistance programs and the number of those who are dependent on them. What's the attraction? They pay every day, and who wouldn't want that!

While writing this portion of the post, I decided to looked up day-hire companies and found several of them, from Washington state to Texas. I, however, did not find them in every state. The companies I did find offered a wide range of various occupations and types of skills they are looking for. Originally I thought that there had to be a specific need, product, trade, etc., but now I see that day-employers hire all sorts of workers for all sorts of industries. From agricultural services, to catering, to janitorial services, to marine services/waterfront manual laborer, to special events and even truck driving. I would doubt that anyone would get bored with their jobs if they had the freedom to work in one area one day, and another the next. I'm sure Human Resources would be a nightmare but there are ways to do anything if it's truly desired. I hope with the turnaround in the job market, day-workers could become a part of the workforce.

Can people get cash change from food stamps?
Answered June 29, 2016, (revised)

Back in the day (1960-1970), as I remember it, food stamp recipients could receive coin change back. I can't recall ever seeing anyone at the checkout receiving actual paper money back as change. I remember high school kids used to buy things like a pack of gum with a $1.00 stamp a few times until they had enough to buy a pack of cigarettes-true entrepreneurs I'd say!

These days I believe things are monitored more closely–depending on the neighborhood you live in. I personally know of someone who had to serve some jail time for allowing purchases, besides food, to take place in his convenient store.

With the Snap (EBT) card I can't see how that's possible. But I also know that there are ways around dining out and using the EBT card. I think that if some of these places want to take that chance then that's on them. I would think that there's nothing in the world that's worth sacrificing freedom, but we are in a place where it's all about the money, getting all that can get got! The amount of young people sitting in DOC because of temptation can vouch for that. In essence, I haven't seen change given back when an EBT card is used.

How do food stamps correspond with TANF? Are they the same thing? If not, how?

Answered July 2, 2016, (revised)

Food stamps and TANF go hand in hand. Once someone signs up to receive public assistance, i.e. a mother or father with children, she will receive the amount of food stamps for her household size, and a certain amount of "cash benefit" also, depending on the size of her household. So a family of 5 could receive $760.00 in food stamps and $259.00 in cash assistance on their EBT cards each month for 45 months (life time benefit). Of course if you do not have children, or you are a single male, you would not receive TANF (cash assistance), you would only receive food stamps (EBT/SNAP).

Do You Think that There is a Correlation between Individuals who Receive Food Stamps and the Increase in the Number Patients with Diabetes?

Answered July 6, 2016, (numbers in this post are at the time of this writing).

Years ago I met a lady who I thought was, well, sort of *out of touch*. She was only 10 years older than I was but her ways were a little different from mine. I could definitely tell the difference between my old city ways and her rural ways. This woman was raised on a farm, so her food was fresh; so fresh that let's just say, they didn't name their farm animals (Ewe!).

During one of my visits with her she said, "You know it's in the food. They're putting something in the food. You ever wonder why all of these diseases are popping up? You notice how many people are coming down with diabetes… and young people at that? They're trying to kill poor people." she said. Alrighty then…

Actually I hadn't thought about it but I should have because I have, and have had, several co-workers in their forties who are diabetic. I just thought it ran in their families. When I hear people who are younger than I am, talking about their health an issue, my first inclination is to think that they must be stress out. I know firsthand how stress affects the body and the mind; (my hobby is studying alternative remedies that were passed down from my grandmother, and passed on to her from her mother). This woman's odd comments may have some merit. With whatever they're using to inject, or use as fillers, or whatever… who really knows what we're eating?

Food that is better processed is not cheap, and who's eating poorer qualities of meat and other food products? Folks who cannot afford to buy the good stuff. Working folks who earn just enough **not** to qualify for food stamps, but who don't earn enough to bypass the need to juggle or sacrifice something else just to buy better food. So here are some questions to ponder, and once again, grad students, you-are-welcome.

What is the percentage of middle income individuals who have diabetes, and what do they normally purchase when they do their grocery shopping? What is the percentage of low income individuals who have diabetes, and what do *they* normally purchase when they do their grocery shopping? And I know what you're thinking but no, low income families who qualify for food stamps sometimes opt to purchase name brand or better quality food items. Talk about a kid in a candy store, and I know what I'm talking about because I see it on a daily basis. Age and the level of physical activity are big factors in both cases. It's more popular to believe that younger people are more physically active, so why are younger people being diagnosed with diabetes? Are they really more physically active or more sedentary these days? Could it be the food?

So, for low income individuals or families, is it the lack of having the *means* to purchase better quality food? Or in the case of middle income individuals or families, is purchasing food of lesser quality out of necessity, because of not qualifying for food stamps or the SNAP program, (Supplemental Nutrition Assistance Program), a possible culprit for health issues? Or… could it be that some individuals or families, who qualify for food stamps because of not being employed, be less active as a result of not having employment? I did not say *all* are unemployed, I said some. If being unemployed is a main variable, could it be that with idle time, because of the inability to secure employment; depression, hopelessness, or even boredom sets in, and what better satisfies boredom than munching.

If munching is responsible for weight gain, and weight gain has been attributed as being one of the possible causes of the onset of diabetes, is it because of the amount of good quality food, the amount of poor quality food, the amount of food in excess, or, in some cases, is it the lack of food and proper nutrition?

A family of 8 could qualify for $1,153.00 per month in food assistance. That to me is a whole lot of good eating. I don't know if it's because I grew up in a household that wasn't too far removed from The Depression Era, and the survival techniques that came with it, or if it was learning how to survive as a starving college student, (an added life-long advantage of going to college, I might add), but being able to manage on $50.00 for groceries for the month, (as a single person) I, my friend, have been taught how to survive on little of nothing.

It saddens me when senior citizens tell me they only receive $11.00 or $13.00 a month in food stamps. Yet they smile when they say it because they're glad to even get that sometimes. Just last week an elderly woman said, "Well it buys my coffee for the month." That breaks my heart, and what also breaks my heart is seeing and hearing so many commercials that suggest that the U.S. is fighting hunger. HOW? I'm a big advocate for programs like, "Save the Food", (SAVETHEFOOD.COM), food pantries, soup kitchens, summer lunch programs and school programs that provide food to be taken home for the weekend. It just makes me wonder that with the surplus of food that we have in our country, why are there hungry families? (*See: Plates as Big as States*).

That brings me to this. Just this past weekend, (at the time of this writing) I was doing a Wellness check on a young mother who had just returned home from grocery shopping, (1ˢᵗ of the month). I watched her unload her groceries and I noticed that she purchased frozen pizzas, waffles and Popsicle, surgery cereals, cupcakes and cookies–all name brand. Yes, there was meat, mostly turkey products, which is good and healthy but Turkey is expensive. So here's what will happen the following weekend when I return, she'll tell me that all of her food stamps are gone (remember that a family of 5 receives $760.00), she has four children. I feel confident in saying this because the same thing happened last month and again I will think, "but how?!"

During our time together I observed, well I observe all of the time no matter where I'm working, that she and her children get up, she makes breakfast, they play a little and then she makes lunch, then back outside to play a little more, she makes dinner and so on. The day consists of cooking, eating, playing, watching T.V., and visiting on occasion. Could this have something to do with the number of people who are being diagnosed with diabetes at a noticeable increase? Is it that there is nothing else to do when there is no employment? Okay, I've said enough for now. Hopefully this will give some graduate student a ton of research topics to choose from.

Why would a job application ask about food stamps?
Answered July 6, 2016, (revised).

I haven't come across a job application that asked if the applicant receives food stamps-not in my area. It could be something that's starting to happen in larger areas? I *could* see a potential employer asking if someone receives TANF (Temporary Assistance to Needy Families/cash assistance) because the applicant could help the potential employer receive a tax credit for the new hire.

The same would hold true if the potential hire was in a subsidized employment placement first. This means agreeing to continue to receive TANF assistance by completing the required hours of participation, (receiving job training) by way of being placed in subsidized employment, (where the state pays the wages for a period of time.)

What are the benefits of the welfare state?
Answered July 7, 2016, (revised).

In a nutshell, one of the main advantages of welfare states is upheaval deterrence. Those who cannot provide for themselves can receive what they need via assistance from their states. Changes have started to take place regarding the length of time families can receive TANF and various other types of assistance, however major changes, especially when it comes to reductions in amounts and services, will need to be done incrementally in order to avoid tension, resistance and retaliation.

What will an employer think of an applicant with an engineering degree currently working fast food?

Answered July 7, 2016

I would think that the potential employer would realize that you are willing to work *anywhere* while you are seeking employment in your field. That shows them that you are not just sitting back waiting for the magic to happen. I would also think that your ambition would land your application/resume in the "interested" pile.

I tell the individuals I work with, (and the same holds true with grant writing), there are several piles that your paperwork could end up in. Where you *don't* want it to end up in is in the "not interested" pile.

Does welfare help poor people without children in the US?

Answered July 10, 2016, (revised).

A single person with no children, and based on income could receive $192.00 per month in food stamps. Individuals who receive food stamps also qualify for the food pantries or food banks. I do remember that back in the 1990's, there was a program that was called General Assistance, (G.A.). It awarded men, (I'm not sure about women) $125.00 per month cash, (well, via a check) plus a voucher for $25.00 that was used to purchase toiletries. But… the men would have to complete ten hours per week doing something in the way of work in order to receive it. I remember one young man who had to help with the remolding and cleanup of a church.

One of the changes that have recently occurred in our area is that if the applicant does not receive disability, is not a senior citizen, has no excuse for not working but live in a household that receives food stamps, the food stamp amount for the family will be reduced.

What needs to be done to reform social welfare?
Answered July 12, 2016, (numbers were at the time of this writing).

In order to continue to revamp social welfare programs, we need to revert back to requiring that something is done in exchange for the benefits received. Currently, a 25% reduction in cash benefits occurs if the individual refuses to complete the required amount of hours agreed upon to receive benefits. For example, $59.50 will be deducted (sanctioned) from the monthly payout of $289.00. Seven out of ten times when I mention sanction I would hear, "Do what you have to do!" In essence, the reduction is more acceptable than putting in the hours in exchange for the full amount of monthly assistance.

The recipient is made aware, at the time of signing up for assistance, that they need to either participate in job searching, or participate in a placement, (where they show up for the required amount of hours at a business and the hours are *worked* off), or even better, participate in a subsidized *employment* placement where not only do they retain their full monthly monetary benefit, they are also paid an hourly wage. In the latter case, they stand a good chance of being hired by the business because they've already received training, plus, the business owner did not have to pay their wages during the time they were in the subsidized placement at their business.

Even though there's a higher rate of success, (there's another one for you grad students) via subsidized employment placements, some of the subsidized workers still end up leaving their placements before the end of the assignment. Our assistance programs have made waking up to an alarm clock way too difficult.

On the plus side, there are also individuals who get tired of being hounded about not keeping up their end of the bargain to receive assistance. They sometimes choose to walk away from assistance programs. I applaud them, if they don't want anyone else calling their shots for them, they could opt to avoid assistance programs at all costs. If they want to hold on to their independence, don't get used to depending on something else in order to survive. I've seen people walked away from public assistance, go to work, and maintain employment at the same place for three or more years. These are the same individuals who tell us that public assistance isn't worth the bother.

When I was a kid signing up for assistance was the worst thing imaginable. Young mothers would rather turn to their families than to have to sign up for assistance. It brings to mind the movie *Claudine,* (Claudine, 1974) and how difficult it was to survive on public assistance, so much so that you just didn't want too. As a matter of fact, Hilton-Jacob's character was against the growing dependence on the welfare system even way back then. Now it's just a walk in the park, albeit the longer wait times to start receiving it. Today there are really not many downsides to welfare programs, not like there used to be. That's why they are so easy to become dependent on.

So, to promote welfare reform just lay the cards on the table. I believe that if we want to encourage accountability for receiving services, the hours need to be completed in order to receive them, (unless there is a disability that prevents this). Move beyond just penalizing by reduction, no hours, no services! There are plenty of businesses out there who would welcome those who don't mind showing up and putting in hours. Yes, there are a few kinks that would need to be ironed out but it would be less costly in the long run. Second, history repeats itself. Making welfare programs *not worth the bother* could result in a decrease in numbers.

Technically one pretty much has to give up everything that has any monetary value in order to receive assistance. Why then, do I see homes that are so nicely furnished they could be featured in magazines, or electronics that I could only wish for, or vehicles galore when I do wellness checks on families? At one time, even purchasing a toaster oven would have to be explained.

If we could get a handle on the generational use and abuse of public assistance programs, we could start redirecting assistance dollars, get people up and out again and stop funding perpetual vacations. And don't think that there are no programs out there that move people up and out of poverty because there are. They are not being enforced as much as they could be. Maybe we could start looking at public assistance programs like we do unemployment. If one has worked and paid in, one could receive assistance before those who have chosen assistance programs as careers.

If a person moves to a different state do they immediately stop snap benefits in that state?

Answered July 12, 2016, (revised).

I'm assume you are asking will your SNAP (food stamps) immediately cancel in the state you are moving from? Social Service workers would love for clients to give a *heads up* when they are planning to move to another state. Does it happen? Well... It may take a little longer for the old state to catch on, but the minute you sign up in the new state the chain reaction starts and your old state is notified.

If you could plan your move just prior to the first of the month, (check your new state's guidelines) while keeping in mind the surge in the number of people on food stamps now, you could apply at the first of the month in your new state. Hopefully you will have enough food left over from your current month to carry you through until your new food stamp case becomes active. Also bear in mind; it may take over a month before you are approved for food stamps in your new state. Your case may move along more quickly if you are physically residing in a shelter or if you have just experienced a fire or flood. In all cases however, proof will have to be provided when requesting emergency food stamps.

It does not end well for those who try to receive food stamps in multiple states although folks have tried. Not only will your food stamps be reduced until the loss is recovered, but as things have started to change, you could face more serious consequences that may result in the loss of SNAP benefits completely and permanently. Just as some states currently have life-time food stamp/public housing bans for felons, I wouldn't be surprised if food stamp programs undergo a complete overhaul with more consequences if fraud is perceived should welfare reform keep moving forward.

Why do governments give people money to have children?
Answered July 25, 2016, (revised).

Initially I believe the plan was to show that we were strong enough in our economy that we are very well capable of providing for our citizens. I feel that after the depression, the powers that be never wanted our society to experience anything like that again. Therefore efforts were made to assure that families, especially indigent families, were taken care of.

I don't know where the notion came from that monthly benefits should increase as family sizes increased. That, in my opinion was the beginning of our downfall, and sadly I recently read, that this could be in the works to happen again?

I realize that this may not be a satisfactory answer to your question, however, I've added a link concerning the decision to reinstate cap-less welfare assistance programs, https://www.msn.com/en-us/money/.

What is the meaning of "welfare catering"?

Answered July 26, 2016, (revised).

"Welfare Catering" is an extension of public assistance that provides services for senior citizens and the disabled who fall within the income guidelines. Some of these services include; shuttle services that provide transportation to and from doctor's appointments.

Others include legal services, tax preparation services, health care services, family care-giver services, (for those who are caring for a senior family member), nutrition services such as "Meals on Wheels" or reduced priced hot lunches at senior Nutrition Centers.

Senior employment services such as "Grandparents" and school-aide helpers, for the growing number of seniors who find that they need to return to the workforce, are also considered to be a form of welfare catering or low income based assistance programs.

What are the requirements for being given welfare money in the US?
Answered July 27, 2016, (revised).

In order to receive public assistance in most states/counties, the applicant has to meet certain criteria prior to completing the actual application. The applicant must be a U.S. resident, a U.S. National, a legal alien, or a permanent resident. They must have very low income, working for very low wages, be unemployed or about to become unemployed, (as in an upcoming lay-off).

Applicants can also be pregnant or be responsible for a child under the age of 18, however if the child will graduate high school prior to their 19th birthday, the child should not jeopardize an approval decision.

Determination of benefits also takes into consideration assets. Owning anything of value, (i.e. more than one house, more than one vehicle or having checking and saving accounts that are above the monetary limit) will also be taken into consideration as part of the determination calculation.

If the applicant goes to the website for the Department of Social Services or the Department of Family Services, (however it is titled in their state/county), there should be a pre-screening eligibility tool where the applicant can enter in their information prior completing the application. This eligibility tool should let the applicant know ahead of time if they are over income or are ineligible to receive cash assistance. Please note that mandatory drug testing could be required as part of the application process if it is deemed necessary, or is required by your state. Any prior drug related offenses/arrests, within a certain time frame, most probably will cause the application to be denied.

How much welfare fraud is there really?
Answered July 28, 2016, (revised).

Welfare fraud is nothing new and I'm sure the powers that be consistently work to try to identify welfare fraud. Even though there is a hotline number that can be called to report fraud, the only times I have had to deal with it was when there was some sort of domestic issue where one is telling on the other to get back at them, or one girl is mad at another girl and is trying to get her in trouble.

The problem is man or woman power, or the lack there of. With budget cuts the way they are, or in the near future may begin to be, there are not enough workers to effectively handle instances of welfare fraud the way they were handled back in the day. With the number of people receiving public assistance now, trying to monitor each and every case to identify welfare fraud would be like trying to carry four dozen loose eggs in your arms at one time-it can't be done, well at least not easily that is.

Back in the 1980's, a dear friend of mine who received public assistance in one form or another for the majority of time I had known her shared with me, "We'll just find another way to get it!" How prophetic she was because the number of individuals who receive disability income has grown astronomically since then. In addition, I have never seen so many children on disability as I do now. (Grad students, interesting research topics. What are some of the reasons children are qualifying for disability payments in the past 5-7 years? Or, what percentage of disability cases in children is granted based on behavioral issues?)

Can I get food stamps if I am on unemployment?
Answered July 28, 2016

Yes, as a matter of fact it should be easier for you to receive food stamps because it will be easier for them to verify your income. Our food stamp office verifies unemployment benefits via the same state system they use to determine food stamp eligibility. They are able to view work quarters and the date unemployment payouts began.

Income, or the lack of income, has to be verified as part of the food stamp application process. In our area, emergency food stamps can also be requested. Do a search to find out if there are any food banks (pantries) in your area. Once you are approved to receive food stamps, you automatically qualify for food bank distributions.

THERESA DIITI

Do Americans pay more taxes than European citizens and if so do Americans have worse social welfare programs?

Answered August 9, 2016, (revised).

I'm not sure what sort of taxes European countries pay, but that is a very good question. I would love to know exactly where my tax dollars go, especially when it comes to funding assistance programs and other social services. I would not consider our welfare programs as being *worse;* in fact they are sometimes so enticing that the benefit can outweigh those obtained from working.

I do however see that our welfare programs can sometimes have a negative effect on the population. They have a tendency to encourage dependency on the programs over self-sufficiency.

In my opinion, this in the end does more harm than good when it comes to helping people who receive public assistance. The skills, or the desire to obtain or use skills for that matter, needed for families to sustain themselves after prolonged dependency on welfare or assistance programs, could be severely hampered if not completely diminished.

If one is not able to survive outside of assistance programs and services, there will be a portion of the population that will not be able to manage, thus resorting to getting their needs met anyway they can.

As long as our welfare programs continue to support those who receive their services for prolonged periods of time, especially from one generation to the next, there will continue to be a need to appropriate a portion of tax dollars to support and maintain assistance programs.

Why has the use of food stamps (SNAP) in the US grown so significantly in the past few years?
Answered August 18, 2016, (revised).

At the time of this initial writing, job loss, higher than usual unemployment, and businesses continuing to close left employees who were used to working with no choice other than to turn to any form of assistance that was available. The above are just a few reasons why there has been an increase in the number of new families applying for food stamps in the past few years.

I chose issues relating families where employment, or the lack thereof, had been impacted over non-working families, (who may have receive food stamps from one generation to the next), because of the mindset when it comes to the decision to apply for food stamps or other assistance programs. When frustration arises due to no longer being employed for instance, and there is now a need to apply for food stamps, new applicants who have never had to use food stamps before might view applying for them in one of two ways. They may prefer not to have to apply for them to begin with, or they may feel that applying for them is justly deserved because portions of their tax dollars have supported food stamps and other assistance programs.

Signing up for food stamps has shifted more toward, "If you can't beat them, join them" in the past several years. This feeling of helplessness or hopelessness mainly happens due to feelings of frustration. When necessities like food can barely be purchased because other bills need to be paid, backs are against the wall; therefore applying for food stamps for working families who have never had to do so in the past, can be quite overwhelming. This adds to the number of new cases applying for food stamps, but what other options are there?

It was not unusual for a frustrated individual sitting across from me to exclaim, "Well how come so-and-so down the street gets…", or "My neighbors have been using the system for years and I'm tired of not making it, so I'm signing up for help too." As well as, "How come I only get this amount when so-and-so gets…", or even, "Why don't I qualify for food stamps when I have worked and worked…" The latter tears my heart out because that, in my opinion, is an example of being punished for working.

Are Headstart programs and other gov funded pre-schools a waste of money—just another liberal ideal turned into a joke?

Answered August 22, 2016, (revised).

Interesting study, thanks for including it. (Head Start Advantages Mostly Gone by 3rd Grade), Study Finds - By Lesli A. Maxwell on December 21, 2012 10:45 AM http://blogs.edweek.org/edweek/early_years/2012/12/head_start_advantages_mostly_gone_by_third_grade_study_finds.html).

I'm curious to find out though what the other "early-childhood programs", that was included in this study, consisted of. I'd also liked to know if each of the programs involved taught/covered the same areas of study, used the same methods of behavioral structuring and communication skills development, etc. Were the other early childhood programs religious based, (Christian Head Start), or head starts that were part of a parent/employee benefit package?

Low income-based head start programs, in my opinion, are one of the few programs that fall under the public assistance umbrella that should avoid the chopping block should there ever be one. Children from low income families need to participate in anything and everything that promotes advancement, and sometimes in low income families, opportunities that promote educational advancement inside the home is non-existent.

You have to remember, in a good number of cases where the parent left school in the seventh, eighth, or ninth grade, the parent is probably not equipped to help their children excel in school, or to even help develop social skills for that matter. Head start programs are sometimes a disadvantaged child's only resource for developing early cognitive, language and social skills. And in some cases, it's the only form of stability, routine and structure these children are exposed to.

THERESA DIITI

Why doesn't the government give food stamps to families suffering from child hunger?

Answered August 22, 2016, (revised).

This question confuses me a bit. Our government does indeed give food stamps to low income families. In addition to food stamps, there are food pantries that operate on various days of the week throughout the month. (See your local Food Banks' monthly calendar to find out when food pantries are open for food distribution, and in addition, when and where the mobile food pantries are available for food pick-up.) The amount allocated for each household member, in my opinion is ample if not more than ample, to feed families for the entire month if managed properly.

Every time I see a television commercial or hear a radio advertisement about children not getting enough to eat, it puzzles me and makes me wonder, "Why are there hungry children?" There's no reason for a child in the U.S. to be hungry unless food, stamps, and other food distribution resources are not being used properly... Humm! Mind you, there is one television commercial that's an exception and something I have seen more often than I'd like to. In the commercial the mother is a school teacher, but what she earns from working is not enough to cover all of the expenses *and* purchase an ample amount of groceries for the month. So we can assume that her teacher's salary makes her ineligible to receive food stamps, and it probably also disqualifies her from receiving other services that could be just a little boost to help her meet all of her monthly obligations.

This is an issue that I'd like to see addressed and remedied because it falls under being *Punished for Working*.

This is why we see individuals that we place in subsidized employment get discouraged after our contract is up with them. It's time for them to fly solo and maintain their employment on their own but it's just too difficult. They no longer qualify for the additional assistance they were receiving prior to being placed at a worksite, be it financial, childcare assistance, reduced rent, utility payments and/or food assistance. Soon after, we see them giving up their jobs and returning to sign up to receive public assistance again. It's just too difficult to try to survive without the assistance they were receiving prior to accepting the job placement.

What I see is poor SNAP management. This is why we are trained to offer classes in meal preparation, budgeting, using coupons to save money on groceries, etc. We hope to encourage SNAP recipients to budget the assistance they receive, take advantage weekly sales at grocery stores, and to be creative with meal planning, (making more than one meal with meat purchases for example). When these practices are put into place, everyone in the household can eat, and eat well at that.

Unfortunately, even though we try to make the classes fun, classroom attendance is never as good as we had hoped that it would be. This could be because the classes are not mandatory. I get a feeling that in the future; classes such as these will be made mandatory in order to continue to receive SNAP benefits. This is why I continue to add to the Life Skills classes I teach, so that the attendees that actually don't mind being there, and futuristically, those who must attend, can get as much out of the classes while hopefully sharing their own pointers. This could help everyone stretch their SNAP benefits and enjoy themselves in class at the same time.

In closing, I feel the need to share that what I have seen is a great deal of food wasted and the attitude of the younger food stamp recipients hints at, "Mind your own business." Lessons learned from having had a grandmother who grew up during the great depression taught me to be as thrifty as I possibly can. Who knows, those who don't seem to feel it necessary to be mindful of tomorrow, (when it relates to food) might get a chance to learn how to appreciate any food they can get in the near future.

Why do people turn criminal? We can feed them with welfare?
Answered August 22, 2016, (revised).

Why, for that matter, do people sometimes take more than what they actually need? Could it be because it's there? Take children, well not literally, but if you leave a huge bowl of candy out and you haven't trained the child that they don't need to take handfuls of it, or to just take one and leave some for someone else, they'll take as much as they can. I don't think it's always a matter of being hungry as the initiator for committing a crime; some folks commit crimes just because. I'm sure there are criminal justice studies out there, (and if not, grad students here's another one for you), that examines the motives for committing crimes. I'm curious to learn how many of them list being hungry as the reason. I'm sure there are a percentage of them that might suggest just that, however I would assume that the numbers would be lower than those listing other reasons for committing crimes.

I truly believe that a good number of crimes are committed out of greed, more so than need (my opinion). Unfortunately, we have become a very greed society, and unfortunately our welfare programs have helped this along. Another way of looking at it is that in my area, a lot of crimes are committed because of addiction. That would be a good study as well, hanging out in courthouses and looking at the dockets to see what people are in court for (if listed). Or, for that matter, asking public defenders if they tally the types of crimes their caseloads consist of, (they might be able to provide an answer right off the bat).

In my opinion, (and I have to say, "In my opinion"), I don't really believe that crimes are being committed because people are hungry. The purposes of our food stamp programs, food pantries, school lunch programs and school food care packages, (so that children who qualify/low income/with a financial need, don't go hungry over the weekend), are to alleviate hunger. As for families who don't qualify for food stamps, there are other resources out there that may be able to provide food packages depending on where you live. I've seen billboards that read, "Need food? Call 555-1212", so food, or the lack thereof, shouldn't be responsible for higher crime rates... unless something happens where we find ourselves in some sort of catastrophe, (see What Would be the Chain of Events if the United States Decided to Abruptly Stop Providing AFDC or Public Assistance?).

I feel that crime rates are bolstered by having nothing to do. An idle mind.... Sure the unemployment rate, (at the initial time of this writing that is, now it seems to be getting better these days; see closing statement), is responsible for folks getting frustrated and tired of even trying; I get that! The propensity to commit crime could depend on the individual, the community they live in, how they grew up, etc. I mean, if it's a family tradition to hot-wire and drive off with as many cars as you can in a day, (career choice), one might tend to lean that way just because it's a familiar way of making money.

Regarding the previous statement about the unemployment rate, because I enjoy hearing people's opinion on current topics, I found myself in the middle of a landmine regarding the decline in unemployment rates and who was really responsible for them. I had no idea that I would get such a backlashing from those who felt that the upward swing for those finding employment was not because of the current administration but the previous administration-jeesh!

What is the success rate of work-based welfare programs?

Answered 24, 2016, updated from original post.

Going back through my posts prior to submitting for publication, I had to rethink some things regarding the original August 24, 2016 entry. In revisiting the post, I discovered that I had not really answered the question.

The question was not, what is the success rate of getting client's to take advantage of work-based welfare programs? It was, "What is the success rate of work-based welfare programs?" There's a difference and I sort of combined the two.

The answer of course varies greatly from state to state, city to city and county to county. I would have to say that in my experience (and I say in my experience often when I write because different caseworkers have different experiences), those who took part in, and completed the work-based (job placement) component of the program, did, and are doing quite well, compared to those who refused a job placement. To date, they have managed to successfully maintain employment, either at their placement site, or they have moved on to another place of employment. Still the result is that they took advantage of what the program had to offer and used it as it was intended.

Therefore the group who actually accepted and completed the job or work-based placement (and I say group and not sample because in the original post, I used rough numbers in my example), had a high rate of success. I feel confident in saying a nearly 90% success rate over those who chose not to accept the work-based component of the program.

Original post August 24, 2016

That covers a broad spectrum; it depends on the number you're starting from. Of course different areas vary, and larger cities have more opportunities for placements where clients can work off their state assistance than smaller cities. The powers-that-be have taken all of this into consideration and have it figured out regarding the expected outcome numbers for each area. I, however, will still try to give you an example. Let's say I have 137 clients on my caseload, 25 of them (a low percentage, but at the time of this writing, accepting a job placement was not mandatory–it was more of a coaxing), will take a placement (work-based welfare placement). They will go to work for a company that has agreed to work with us by providing our clients with a work-site.

Ten of the 25 will go on to secure permanent employment, either by becoming a permanent employee at their placement site, or by securing employment on their own. In both cases, if they think about it, they were able to secure permanent employment because they had employment (even if it was temporary) – now there's a thought! Of course after the time limit has been reached regarding placements, those who were not successful in securing permanent employment (15 let's say), would circle back into the client pool which is now back up to 127.

Twenty of the remaining 127 might get sick of us bugging them and ask to be taken off of assistance because they had no intention of accepting a job placement via our program, but after a couple of months we'll see them again. Ironically, 3 of that twenty are part of the "Gotcha" group. They were so easy to give up their assistance because they had already started working, but they felt the need to withhold this information for a while for fear of losing assistance (and they would eventually lose some, if not all, of their assistance once we stepped aside because they were now gainfully employed).

So that leaves 107. Let's say that half of the 107 have children under a certain age so they are not required to start looking for work yet. The remaining half is responsible for caseworkers questioning their own existence in this world. This group houses the entrepreneurs of our time though because they manage to create ways to survive with what they receive via assistance (as far as we know). If you need reasons for not working, they can give you some in no time flat. Sometimes, I believe their motto is, "I don't wake up to alarm clocks and I don't live by punching time clocks."

Back to the point though, sometimes they present some valid reasons for not agreeing to a job placement, but the cost of child care doesn't really get it anymore because childcare is paid for when they accept the work-based placement. Not caring for some of the childcare providers on the list however is valid, and in my opinion, we can't dismiss that.

So just by using this example and numbers, less those parents who are not required to work yet, and those who told us to get lost, I could roughly say that the percentage of assistance recipients who actually and successfully utilize the job placement component is approximately 9.35% (of my original base number 137). That's a low percentage when it comes to doing something that could change a life or a household. It also leaves a high enough number of folks we're responsible for who aren't improving, while leaving a good number of caseworkers who want to hurl themselves out into oncoming traffic.

What are the dangers of a welfare state?
Answered September 7, 2016, (revised).

The dangers of Welfare states are their tendency to encourage dependence versus independence. States that make applying for, and receiving public assistance an easy process, fail to realize that they become appealing to those who would rather use less effort and not work in order to survive. This, in my opinion, takes away the ability to view employment as the best way to care for self and family.

Please keep in mind that I come from a place where the majority of the families on my client-loads have depended on the welfare system for generations. So when I write, it's mainly based on my experiences of working with those families who have been involved with the welfare system for generations. It appears that our assistance programs have not discouraged being on welfare because the younger of these generations, who grow up depending on public assistance, most times, end up turning to one form or another of public assistance themselves. (Of course, any assistance that helps to continue education and training, or helps to make child support payments is a different story, that's not what I'm talking about here.)

Well think about it! If you don't have to worry about how you're going to eat, or heat your apartment or house, that turns into part of a child's training as they grow up. Your parents wanted you to be able to take care of yourself and your children just as they did for you, through whatever means available. **But,** when dealing with those who have depended on public assistance programs for generations, as a means of survival over working, the missing link is *employment*. There's not a lot of assistance out there if you're employed, especially if you're employed full-time so why do it?

Assistance programs for these families are sometimes viewed as a form of employment, because they, like employment, help to sustain life. If this is what children see and come to accept as a way to survival as well, why is there a need to secure employment as they become adults? They realize that they can sustain on what they already receive, and that their basic needs are being met via assistance programs. To give all of this up and go to work? That's much less appealing and less likely to happen.

Welfare states confuse ways of thinking from what I've seen. I sometimes get looks that seem to suggest, why would I want to make my life harder by working?

I have actually had clients tell me that they are moving to this state or that state because they pay out more in public assistance, yet they are not moving there because there are more job opportunities. I believe this is the reason why we might start to see changes in how assistance is doled out in the future and I rest my case!

What would be the chain of events if the United States decided to abruptly stop providing AFDC or public assistance?
February 16, 2018, (revised).

I don't believe that the *powers-that-be* would make such drastic decisions or changes like that. They are well aware of what would happen and they are aware of the percentage of the population who are not able to take care of themselves. I would hope that they are also aware that welfare programs have not turned out the way they were originally expected to.

The inception of welfare programs have mainly occurred because of unfortunate tragedies affecting our economy and stability, (depression, recession, loss of jobs, etc.) They are implemented to ease pressures until we can move past these tragedies. However, evidence in the past, that something needed to be done to make people aware that programs such as welfare were *temporary,* became apparent when time limits to receive these benefits were put into place.

There will always be individuals and families who need of some sort of assistance, but abruptly stopping welfare could cause pandemonium. First, keep in mind that a percentage of the percentage of those who receive welfare assistance and food stamps were employed at one time, or are currently under-employed. To take away from those who have worked and paid in would be unfair. They are just receiving a fraction of what they have already contributed. I would expect to see unrest from that portion of the overall percentage of recipients, and rightfully so.

Another portion of the percentage (generational), those who are not accustomed to getting their needs met outside of receiving welfare, well, they will perform-it will be show time! They will find ways to justify their anger for losing their public assistance. There most probably would be protests and riots, even in instances where nothing has been paid in to help support said welfare assistance programs by the individuals who are doing the protesting and rioting.

In regards to rioting (and yes there would be plenty if we're talking about taking assistance programs away), I get the mental image of someone asking, "Why are we protesting and rioting?" with the response being, "I'm not sure but it's exciting, let's do it!"

What are some good arguments against welfare?
Answered September 10, 2016, (revised).

Oh why did you ask this? From my perspective, welfare does more harm than good, (for some that is). In my opinion, and from what I have actually seen, welfare seems to cause laziness; it hinders responsibility, or in my experience as a caseworker, it makes being responsible less appealing. The result seems to be a dependence on a "system" that one day may not be as generous, (at least not in the way it is now). Most times I hear, when trying to discourage individuals from remaining on assistance, "I'll deal with not having it if that time ever comes." In other words, mind your own business; I'm not getting off of it.

I look at welfare as a system that leads folks to the slaughter. And yes, there are families on welfare who have never been on it before, nor did they think they would ever have to apply for it. They are usually the applicants who will only have to accept public assistance for a short period of time, and they most likely will not have to apply for *temporary* assistance again. These are also the applicants who are not saying "NO" to employment opportunities that present themselves via welfare-to-work services.

Welfare, in its various forms, has also started to become attractive to folks who are just fed up with barely getting by. I hear more folks say, "Why not sign up for it? Everyone else is." Of course *everyone* is not signing up to receive assistance, but more folks are on it now, or at least receive food stamps.

I see more working people give up on "trying to make it" because things are getting more expensive and their earnings are not going as far as they once did, (being *punished for working*). Are grocery store prices increasing because more people are on food stamps and not paying cash for their food anyhow? What does this mean for the people who are not on food stamps?

We have to make choices when it comes to making purchases, (it's either this or that, but not both these days). Or we have to completely do without while others are getting by and doing just fine without having to do anything for it. It's a kick in the teeth and it makes one wonder, *is that right?*

What a lot of the folks I work with are not seeing, is that helplessness or hopelessness is replacing their drive to succeed independently. Welfare has caused them to turn over their own well-being to the state-or whatever funding source they have come to depend on. A source that to me, is not as stable as they have led themselves to believe. This source could also start to dry up in the future, or at least be reduced to accommodate other areas within the infrastructure.

How can you use food stamps if you are traveling out of state?
Answered September 12, 2016

You would use your food stamps (SNAP cards) just like you do in your home state because they are accepted in all fifty states. If you are just visiting, you can use your SNAP card for purchases, but I believe that once you are in the new state for more than thirty days, (depending on that states residency rules) you may need to declare your new residency, close your old food stamp case and apply for a new SNAP card in the new state.

Can you buy wine with food stamps?

Answered September 26, 2016

You cannot purchase alcoholic beverages or tobacco products with food stamps (SNAP card). I have heard of a business, and I'm sure this place of business is not the only one, where the owner was accepting them to pay for anything in his store. Needless to say, he is currently in prison so was it worth it?

That said, you raise an interesting question. Cooking wines and Sherries, to my knowledge can be purchased with food stamps. Even though both of them are not drinkable, they still have some alcohol in them if only in minuscule amounts. Humm…

How does welfare disincentivize work?

Answered October 24, 2016, (revised).

Years have passed since I answered this question. I'm in the process of updating all of my posts and this one is first. I'd like to adjust this question; why is it so hard to move from welfare (public assistance) to work?

Welfare dis-incentivizes work because there are more tempting *incentives* to sign up for it. And from what I've seen, this makes working seem less appealing, especially for those who are not used to working in the first place. For the currently unemployed however, especially due to COVID 19, public assistance is sometimes the only alternative. Therefore, people who have lost their jobs should be moved to the front of the line to receive the help they need, and the much needed *temporary* relief should be awarded without hesitation. From my experience, those who possess *a working mindset* are less likely to ask for help, and they usually don't develop a long-term dependence on public assistance. Getting back to work is almost always the main goal.

Problems occur when it becomes easier to live on welfare than it does to live on earned wages; thus making it easier for dependence on welfare to set in. We work to meet our basic needs and wants, and we're usually pretty happy when payday rolls around so that we can tend to those needs and wants. Welfare also takes care of basic needs (sustenance), and judging by some of the purchases I see being made using the cash portion of EBT cards, it also takes care of some wants-even if it's only just a few of them. Welfare wasn't designed to make folks wealthy, (well there was a case or two back in the day but they should be out of prison by now).

Welfare was designed so that food can be purchased (Food Stamps), as well as items needed to survive until the next month (the cash portion of TANF for personal items, diapers, household products, etc.) In both cases, food stamps and TANF are indeed meeting some of the wants and needs of those who receive them.

The difference between working and living on welfare is that with most jobs, we usually have to be at a place, (even if it's in front of a computer screen) by a certain time, at least some days out of a week. But with welfare (less the TANF work/volunteer component), there isn't a required time to be at any place, by any certain time on any day of the week. The freedom of having all the time you want, to do whatever you want, (within your financial means that is) is what I would call a big incentive that disincentivizes work.

There are quite a few incentives that go along with receiving welfare. Along with free food and a little cash if you qualify for the cash assistance, you could also qualify to receive help with paying your light and gas bills. In some areas, a household could receive $1,400.00 or more per year to pay their power bills. The recipient does not receive the cash; the power company does. If managed correctly though, this could cover at least 6 months of utility payments, leaving the money saved from not having to pay light and gas bills, to be used for other things. (For tightwads like me, it would stretch even further.) Now if that's not a welfare incentive, I don't know what is.

There are disagreements with this however; with the argument being that power companies and grocery stores raise their prices because the state or government is paying for it anyhow, not the consumer. But what does that mean for those of us who are not on welfare; we are the paying consumers who get stuck with paying the higher prices.

Medicaid for free medical services is another incentive for welfare recipients. Working individuals who work for low wages, as I do, do have the option of

Obama care (or the Marketplace) for medical insurance, but we still have to pay what insurance doesn't, our doctor's visits are not free by any means.

Households who receive food stamps and have school aged children could get internet services for $10.00 per month. One of the major cell phone companies offers this service to low income families who meet their criteria and have elementary school children in the home - another incentive.

I'd like to share a little blurb from a few years ago when I provided services for a young man who was a farm worker. Although he would be returning to work in the next few months, any money he had saved had been depleted. He and his wife decided that it would be better if she left her part-time job because it would reduce their income to zero. Their rationale was, with no income, they would qualify for more assistance to pay for things they simply could not afford to pay now that his employment had ended for the season.

They could receive all of the benefits available for low-income families such as food stamps and Medicaid, there would be no childcare expenses because they were both home now, and their upcoming higher winter utility bills could also be paid. With no income they could even qualify for donated Christmas baskets for their kids. As you can see, some of the perks make working and barely getting by seem futile.

When receiving some forms of public assistance, the recipient could choose to complete participation hours, (fulfilling their obligation to complete the required hours in exchange for the benefits they receive from the state and government) via unsubsidized employment, workplace placement (subsidized employment), or volunteering or attending school or training. No matter which of these they choose, they could qualify for paid childcare. When you're not on welfare and working, and you need childcare services, you have to pay for it, and at quite a handsome cost in some cases.

What would happen if the United States cancelled all social welfare?
Answered October 25, 2016, (revised).

I sincerely doubt welfare will ever completely go away, although some reductions have already started to be put in place-once again. The first change that I can remember hearing anything about was the Personal Responsibility and Work Opportunity Reconciliation Act of 1996, (PRWORA) signed by then President Bill Clinton. This Act was responsible for creating TANF (Temporary Assistance for Needy Families). TANF set time limits for families receiving public assistance, plus it added a mandatory work or skills training component.

So versus a family receiving assistance and doing nothing in exchange for receiving it, the hopeful outcome regarding this restructuring was for recipients to start taking advantage of some of the skills enhancement components that went along with receiving TANF. Emphasis was now placed on promoting self-sufficiency and self-responsibility while moving from welfare to work. Instead of leaving families with nothing once they reached their TANF time limits, if they took full advantage of the services offered, (job training, job placement, or even taking GED classes) they should be able to secure employment and become self-sufficient prior to reaching their lifetime limits.

On August 28, 2015 an emergency amendment regarding TANF requirements was added stipulating that new eligibility and work participation requirements be implemented for temporary assistance applicants. Participants in the TA program must meet the new requirements in order to qualify for benefits by participating in work activities. These activities include job seeking or receiving job training, participating in job placements or working 20-30 hours for a full week for a federal month for a single parent household, etc. In addition, on January 1, 2016, family lifetime limits to receive TANF dropped from 60 to 45 months, (this did not affect Food Stamps, Medicaid, etc.)

Although these changes are now in effect, you can see that completely ending welfare is not something that the powers-that-be would do at a moment's notice; it's just not practical. Changes in our welfare system need to be made and changes have started to take place, but they are taking place in increments. Almost on a daily basis I come across situations that allow me identify possible remedies for discouraging the abuse of, and the dependence on, public assistance programs. I try to shed light on some of these remedies in many of my writings.

I share with clients who are long-term public assistance recipients that programs such as TANF and utility assistance programs are not guaranteed to continue to operate the way they have been. Therefore, they need to start taking a serious look at what they could do to start weening themselves off of them. The response is usually, "We'll deal with that when it happens." Well at least they've been given a heads-up.

How much welfare fraud is there really?
Originally Answered: **Is welfare fraud really rampant?**
Answered July 28, 2016 - Updated January 14, 2020.

I had a hard time getting back to this one. It depends on what you mean by fraud and rampant. Do you mean fraud in the application process (honesty) or fraud in the use of welfare, or the sharing of welfare benefits (food stamps)? Rampant meaning how many family members in one extended family are receiving some form of welfare? Rampant in terms of how many generations, in let's say 10,000 families (as a sample), that are receiving long-term welfare benefits? Or do you mean rampant due to the increase in the number of new families that have had to sign up for welfare due to losing their employment? Or rampant because of the number of families who have developed the mindset of, "Oh the heck with it, let's just go and sign up for welfare because everybody else is on it." And yes, I do see the latter more than I'd like to. Folks are just tired of giving 100% and getting nowhere, this makes it easier to feel, "If you can't beat them, join them!"

Fraud during the application process, from what I've seen, is not so easy to commit anymore because of the screening process. But it can still be done because our clients are much smarter than we are in many instances. Unlike "back in the day", we cannot legally walk into someone's home and ask them where they got their new, and expensive at that, washer and dryer off of $237.00 per month in cash assistance. We can't walk through their homes and count the number of HD TV's they have, or mention that every time we see them, their manicures are to die for! Just can't do it!

When welfare, or the idea of having to sign up for it, was less attractive, social workers/case workers could get away asking questions when they saw things in excess, or that could not possibly be obtained with the low income provided by the state. Actually, that was a social workers/case workers job at that time, and because people on welfare didn't like answering the why's and how's, more families chose to avoid signing up for it if at all possible. There were less people were on welfare at that time, but there were more jobs back then too.

The term I hear most often is, "Sold her food stamps." As a matter of fact just a couple of months ago, my dear co-worker, (who had fallen upon hard times and was in the process of being approved to start receiving them) got a phone call from her neighbor who offered her $100.00 of her food stamps. This co-worker knew that any discussion about food stamps, and how they're being abused, makes me welcome the idea of having bamboo shoots shoved under my fingernails, found delight in sharing this news with me. I then found delight in saying, "That's fraud!" Needless to say, I have no proof that she ever accepted her neighbors' food stamps, and if she did, she would never tell me because she knew how I felt about it.

After she had been approved for food stamps, she took pleasure in using the words "food stamps" at least 50 times a day. But, she also adds that she's worked and paid taxes, so her family deserves them. This idea about food stamps has gone viral, and I have no argument with someone who has worked and paid in; but... they usually are not part of the population who are responsible for the abuse of the welfare system either.

Can I have Medicaid and get food stamps too?
Answered November 23, 2016, (revised).

Yes, as a matter of fact it's almost unusual to see someone receiving Medicaid who is not also receiving food stamps. Usually, anything that's considered state assistance is taken care of through one agency (The Division of Social Services or Family Services Division).

At one time, in my area, state funded Child Care, Child Support, Food Assistance, Health Care, Services for the Blind and Temporary Assistance (TANF or Temporary Assistance for Needy Families/cash assistance) were applied for through one major system, (or at least during the beginning of the application process). A good portion of the financial information the applicant provided when they signed up for Medicaid, is the same information Social Services would review for food stamps.

Applications are available on line and can be completed and printed out ahead of time and dropped off, (along with any of the other requested information). The online instructions suggested that the applicant should hear something regarding your approval in one to three months.

Should welfare and food stamps recipients only receive healthy MRE style food, instead of money from the government? Would that save money and reduce the amount of people who abuse that system? Would that encourage people to focus on more work?

Answered Feb 15, 2018, (revised).

Actually MRE style food packages could be more cost effective than the Supplemental Nutrition Assistance Program (SNAP) food stamp cards that are currently being used. I look at it like this, and meaning no disrespect but with the amount of individuals who are selling their food stamps anyhow, replacing a portion of the cash allotment of food assistance with MRE's could prove to be effective in making sure families are possible eating and not profiting as much monetarily from state food assistance programs. What did we use to hear, "When you get hungry enough, you'll eat it!" I do believe that the bulk of assistance programs will start to undergo major restructuring in the future and who knows, distributing MRE's could be on the table.

Hopefully after the Coronavirus has been managed if not completely eradicated, jobs will once again become available in abundance and we should start to see less of a reliance on assistance programs all the way around. In my experience, there have always been ways to get around crackdowns in public aid, but getting people back to work should reduce the amount of people receiving the assistance to abuse in the first place.

I might add that working in this field has allowed me to come into contact with individuals who would prefer to work and not receive assistance at all, but because of the loss of higher paying jobs in our area (plant closings), sometimes, there's no other choice. The other side of the coin seems to sometimes suggest though, that too much will be lost once employment has been secured. Individuals most times are not willing to give up the amount of assistance they receive, thus they choose the path of least resistance and opt out of working.

Why do people sell their food stamps for half the amount they're worth?
Answered Feb 15, 2018, (revised).

People sell their food stamps for half the amount they're worth because they need the cash. But mostly, people sell their food stamps for half the amount they're worth because there are no food stamp police to do anything about it. The individuals buying them are getting more food at a lower cost, and tax free at that. Magic happens when the plastic EBT card turns into cash.

Actually years ago I read where individuals could receive something if they reported the abuse of food stamps. The only time I was informed about any abuse was the time a gentleman was trying to get back at his girlfriend. When I asked if he would be willing to phone the food stamp abuse hotline, he advised that he thought he was calling the hotline and he disconnected the call. When receiving Temporary Assistance for Needy Families, (TANF) and Supplemental Nutrition Assistance Program (SNAP), and let's say there's a "habit", food stamp cash is usually the only source of income to do whatever needs to be done.

I think a good research project would be to interview the people who buy food stamps and the individuals who sell them. Do you think either group of subjects would boldly step forward, waiving their hands in the air saying, "I do I do!" to the questions, "Do you buy food stamps or do you sell your food stamps?" I wouldn't hold my breath, but selling food stamps happens every day somewhere.

My own boss shared once that, "back in the day" when she had food stamps, with 4 children, she did what she had to do! (Unbeknown to her, I'm aware that she still buys them). Once the cash part of cash assistance runs out, food stamp cash is the back up.

Can I get food stamps if I have a P.O box only to get mail?
Answered Mar 21, 2018, (revised).

The applicant has to list a physical address because we are sometimes required to visit the home. Also, our systems are connected, meaning that we check to see if addresses match up. We try to see if there are more than one family or additional family members living in the household. We can also use physical addresses to locate individuals who are listed at different or multiply addresses for the purpose of increasing the food stamp amount.

Why does the department of Social Services ask for my landlord's name and address when applying for TANF and SNAP? Won't that jeopardize my chances of lease renewal if they think I don't have money?
Answered Apr 5, 2018, (revised).

This is a very interesting question. Based on the amount of your rent, DSS (Department of Social Services) can get a clearer picture of what your income actually is by what you can afford to pay your landlord. In our area for example, if you are renting a $600.00 a month apartment, and you were not receiving low income housing assistance, (subsidized) to help you pay your rent, that would be a red flag when applying for TANF and SNAP benefits.

Usually the Department of Social Services is aware of landlords who accept low income, subsidized and section 8 tenants. If by chance your landlord is not already listed as one who accepts state payment for low income tenants, your DSS worker might want to know who your landlord is to verify the amount of your rent payments. The only reason your landlord would decide not to renew your lease is if you were not paying your rent. But let me be clear, there are other reasons why a landlord might decide not to renew a lease and they can be found in another one of my replies, (*Can Evictions be Taken Off?*-March 4, 2018).

I believe your social service worker is just trying to make sure that you haven't misrepresented yourself as being low income when you're not. If you can manage to secure housing with rent payments that are above the low income eligibility guidelines, there might be additional income somewhere that was not reported on your TANF/SNAP application.

You technically should not be able to qualify for TANF and SNAP benefits if you can make sizable unsubsidized rent payments. As long as your landlord continues to get his or her rent on time, he or she should have no problem providing rent verification for the Department of Social Services.

Do people live off welfare?
Answered Jun 6, 2018

In our area yes, people can live off of welfare and do so nicely if they take advantage of all of the other available assistance programs, manage their resources, and take advantage of free recreational activities. Keep in mind, this requires living a very simple and frugal life, but it is possible and I see it every day. For example, if a family receives $259.00 a month in TANF plus their food stamps, and they secure an apartment or house through public housing or Section 8 rental assistance, they're pretty much set for the month.

So an apartment in public housing (Housing Authority) considers a percentage of what the family receives via TANF (this makes rent = $59.00 for example), that leaves $200.00 to live off of for the rest of the month. Some subsidized housing includes utilities, others do not, but for those who have to pay their own utilities, there are Energy Assistance programs that could pay the utility bills. Families who receive TANF are pretty much guaranteed approval for utility assistance, thus $200.00 back in the pocket, (or still on the EBT card). That said, TANF and SNAP (food stamps) go hand in hand, thus no need to worry about money to purchase groceries. But for personal items, and things like cleaning supplies, etc., they can be purchased with the remaining $200.00 on the card. How many times in one month does bleach, floor cleaner, furniture polish, etc., need to be purchased? Dish washing detergent and laundry detergent; I can see maybe but…

For recreation, take the kids to the library where there are free movie and music rental, go to free museums, take advantage of what the parks and recreation has to offer, and in our area, there is music in the park… just bring snacks and a cooler.

One of the classes I teach is money management and we go over how to live off of the monthly state assistance received. It can actually be done using the model of living off of $50.00 per week. You have to remember that if everything else is already paid for the month, and the family doesn't have a lot of places to go (gasoline), it can be done and continues to be getting done.

Why do poor people think food stamps make taxes fair?
Answered July 5, 2018

I have never engaged in conversations about taxes with food stamps or public assistance service clients–it just doesn't mix in an oil and water sort of way. I was however privy to a conversation between a young lady and a coworker both of whom received food stamps. It was lunch time and the young lady suggested that my coworker get her lunch from a nearby convenient store and use her food stamp. "If you use your food stamp card", she continued, "You won't have to pay taxes on your food." I can't remember how far my mouth dropped open, but I'm sure it was noticeable.

I have gotten into minor tiffs about what I feel are misconceptions about public assistance programs being a "right" as some of the service recipients I've worked with suggest. A couple of years ago I was listening to a radio talk show and a woman phoned in with the argument that individuals and families who receive public assistance pay taxes. She went on to say that they do pay taxes on what they purchase. Okay, so am I the only one who sees that although that may be true, they are making-purchases-with-what-they-receive-via-free-state-and-government-money?

Anyhow, the radio discussion was getting pretty heated, and I got busy doing something else so I never found out how it ended, but I could guess. Discussions that include taxes, food stamps and public aid are one of those, "Never going to win" discussions.

Should people who receive government assistance be forced to only have 1 child?

Answered June 13, 2018

I do not believe that limiting the number of children parents could have would be feasible or would ever even be considered in the United States. The limits that have been put in place have nothing to do with the number of children in the household; SB 24 (2015) [67] did however change the time limits to receive public assistance, as well as program requirements.

By working in the field and paying attention, I can pretty much bet there are more changes to come regarding public assistance as a whole. I think more focus may be placed on public assistance fraud for starters.

When you go on public assistance such as welfare or snap, does it become public information?

Answered June 14, 2018

No, not public record so to speak, but some systems are interconnected. I've mentioned in previous answers that the application process includes verifying income. The applicant is required to report all income, (if they have any) as well as identify their income sources.

Let's say you receive unemployment, we would be able to identify the last quarters you worked, that unemployment is your source of income, and the amount you received because the systems are connected, *so to speak*. All income has to be calculated in order to approve the case, to arrive at the correct monthly amount of benefits if approved, or to deny the case.

As far as public record like the court system, or an entry in newspaper, public assistance information is not public record to my knowledge. What is public record are convictions, and depending on the type of conviction, because it is public record, we would be able to locate it and the applicant will not be approved to receive assistance from some programs, (including housing assistance).

Why are food stamps considered public assistance?
Answered Jul 1, 2018, (revised).

I believe it's because it is income based. The food stamp program is designed to assist individuals or families who do not have enough income to purchase the food they need for proper nutrition (as per the Department of Health and Human Services poverty guidelines). Foods stamps or SNAP, (Supplemental Nutrition Assistance Program) falls under the umbrella of public assistance programs. Public assistance programs are federal and state funded and this includes food stamps.

THERESA DIITI

Does installing home office entitle you to food stamps, meals, and transportation?

Answered April 18, 2020

I'm afraid not. Public assistance is for low income households, that's why the application asks you to list your assets to see if you meet or exceed the low income guidelines.

Just the sound of "home office" immediately lets me know that you could possibly be unaware that you are not supposed to own anything of value except a home and one vehicle if you're applying for public assistance. Depending on where you're located, (check your states' Department of Social Services website) at the time you apply for public assistance, (food stamps or TANF); you cannot own anything above the value amount listed on the website. This also includes whatever is in your bank account.

Home offices would consist of equipment that would have to be sold because they are considered to be of value. This is why it's not uncommon to hear, "I have to sell everything I own before I can apply for food stamps? When it comes to meals and transportation, meals-on-wheels and programs like them are also based on income. So if you qualify for food stamps, you could also qualify for home delivered meals. In addition, if you are disabled you are eligible for food stamps and you could also qualify for shuttle services to and from doctor's appointment, grocery shopping, etc.

I do have to ask though, could it be that you have seen or know of someone who claims to be low income, but have, or are planning to install a home office? With everything that's going on right now, it wouldn't surprise me because more people are earning their incomes by working from home. That said, even prior to where we are now, I've seen things in low income homes that have blown my mind.

Does social welfare call your house?

Answered April 13, 2020

Yes, social welfare is required to have some sort of contact, in my area on a monthly basis, with anyone who has signed up to receive TANF, Temporary Assistance for Needy Families. However, monthly contact is not required if you only receive food stamps. The purpose for contacts is to monitor whether or not the recipient is upholding their end of the bargain by completing participation hours. Completing the required weekly or monthly hours is something what was agreed upon at the time of signing up to start receiving TANF.

The number of hours to be completed is based on the ages of the children in the household. Age six and over complete 30 hours per week but if the children are under the age of six, only 20 hours per week needed to be completed. Participating by completing the required number of hours prevents a reduction in TANF amounts.

Participation includes working, (whether on your own or via accepting a worksite placement), volunteering, (which sometimes leads to employment), or attending school or training opportunities. These services are provided to help the recipient receive what they signed up for and in exchange, the recipient advances by participating one of the above. If the recipient opts out of working, they can attend GED classes (which are hard to find these days), or attend a training program (CNA, Carpentry, etc.) at no cost to the recipient.

Participation is monitored by making contact with the worksite or school and via the receipt of the "attendance or time sheets". When this doesn't happen on a weekly/monthly basis, contact needs to be made with the assistance recipient to find out why the agreement is not being upheld (compliance). This is first done via the phone but if this is unsuccessful, an office or home visit follows. The contacts are required because the Federal and State agencies have provided the needed assistance, either monetarily or by paying for education or training to help the recipient improve their circumstances.

CHAPTER 14

Acknowledgments

Bobby, how could you put up with us for so long? Nerves of steel! You watched me grow up from the age of 10, and you have always had faith in me. I will always love and cherish you. Thank you.

Granny, you told me "You can do it; you can do it if you put your mind to it!" I could not have survived if it hadn't been for the lessons that you taught me. Thank you.

Granddaddy, for teaching me that I am just as good as anyone else and that being respectful and always learning can take me wherever I want to go, thank you. I miss you both.

Past elementary (Ms. Chestang, "You'll take the long way home but you'll get there"), and high school teachers, university instructors and professors, and my dear friends Lois and Lucy, I thank you for "understanding me and my weirdness." I will never forget you and your friendship. True and unconditional love and understanding are hard to find.

Cindy D, you heard, you understood, and you had patience, so much patience. You even planted a tree for me and mine; you are truly an angel on earth. Thank you for your shelter, may God pour down many blessings on you and your family.

Bo's J&P, sometimes you just have to do what you have to do! You saved my life a million times. Thank you and God bless you.

Lee, you were always there when I needed you. No matter what, you kept me going, and you were instrumental in helping me get my new start. There is a special place in heaven for you. God bless you.

Social service workers and anyone else who can make a difference in the lives of others by helping them learn how to depend on themselves and not the system, I thank you, too.

Lastly, I just wouldn't feel right if I didn't respectfully mention graduate students. In *Punished for Working*, you'll find a gazillion of potential research topics (hence the repeated refrain, "More research is needed to examine, to conclude, to identify, to propose…").

CHAPTER 15

References

Flagg, E. (2012). http://www.bravotv.com/million-dollar-listing-los-angeles/season-5/episode-9-big-listings-big-losses.

Chapter 3

1. Shipler, D.K. (2004, 2005). The Working Poor. New York, NY: Random House, Inc.

Chapter 4

1. *Peters, Gerhard; Woolley, John T. The Comprehensive Employment and Training Act* (CETA, Pub. L. 93–203). "Statement on Signing the Comprehensive Employment and Training Act of 1973, December 28,

1973". *The American Presidency Project,* retrieved 2012-08-30 December 28, 1973.

2. Cornell Law School, (The Wex Definitions Team). September, 2021. *Three Strikes.* Legal Information Institute. https://www.law.cornell.edu/wex/three_strikes.

3. USA FACTS, September 15, 2022. *How much do states spend on prisons?* https://usafacts.org/articles/how-much-do-states-spend-on-prisons/

Chapter 5

Killosophy: Killing Knowledge. Loving Wisdom. Jami, Criss. January 8, 2015.

1. Snap Eligibility Calculator-Snap Eligibility Apply for Food Stamps Online Makeoverarena. *October 1, 2019.* https://www.makeoverarena.com/snap-eligibility-calculator /

2. *Food Waste and Food Rescue.* Feeding America. https://www.feedingamerica.org/our-work/reduce-food-waste

3. https://insights-engine.refed.org/food-waste-monitor?break_by=sector&indicator=tons-waste&view=detail&year=2019

4. *Food Waste FAQs*. USDA and EPA. U.S. Department of Agriculture Secondary Navigation. 2016. https://www.usda.gov/foodwaste/faqs

5. *What is Sociology?* The University of North Carolina at Chapel Hill. Department of Sociology. https://sociology.unc.edu/undergraduate-program/sociology-major/what-is-sociology/

Chapter 6

1. COVID-19 Food Stamp (SNAP) Benefits Information. Media Release July 28, 2021. https://dss.mo.gov/press/07-28-2021-p-snap-benefits.htm

2. SB 24 Modifies provisions of law relating to the Temporary Assistance for Needy Families Program and the Supplemental Nutrition Assistance Program. CCS/HCS/SS#2/SCS/SB 24 - This act is known as the "Strengthening Missouri Families Act". January 11, 2015. https://www.senate.mo.gov/15info/bts_web/Bill.aspx?SessionType=R&BillID=153

3. Shipler, D.K. (2004, 2005). The Working Poor. New York, NY: Random House, Inc.

4. Nearly 40 Percent of Americans with Annual Incomes over $100,000 Live Paycheck-to-Paycheck. Jun 15, 2021. **https://www.prnewswire.**

com/news-releases/nearly-40-percent-of-americans-with-annual-incomes-over-100-000-live-paycheck-to-paycheck-301312281.html

Chapter 7

1. The Special Supplemental Nutrition Program for Women, Infants, and Children (WIC). July 9, 2022. Food and Nutrition Service. U.S. Department of Agriculture. c/about-WIC. **https://www.fns.usda.gov/wic**

2. Annual Statistical Supplement. 2015. Social Security Office of Retirement and Disability Policy. **https://www.ssa.gov/policy/docs/statcomps/supplement/2015/ssi.html**

3. SSI: A Lifeline for Children with Disabilities. May 11, 2017. Kathleen Romig. https://www.cbpp.org/research/social-security/ssi-a-lifeline-for-children-with-disabilities

Chapter 8

1. Townsend, R. (Director). (2000). *Holiday Heart* [TV Movie]. MGM Television; Tribeca Productions.

2. Salky, A. (Director). (2015). *I Smile Back* [Film]. Broad Green Pictures.

Chapter 9

1. Millions of tenants at risk as federal eviction ban ends. Jul 31, 2021. Hari Sreenivasan/Emily Benfer. PBS News Weekend. **https://www.pbs.org/newshour/show/millions-of-tenants-at-risk-as-federal-eviction-ban-ends**

Chapter 10

1. SB 24 Modifies provisions of law relating to the Temporary Assistance for Needy Families Program and the Supplemental Nutrition Assistance Program. CCS/HCS/SS#2/SCS/SB 24 - This act is known as the "Strengthening Missouri Families Act". January 11, 2015. https://www.senate.mo.gov/15info/bts_web/Bill.aspx?SessionType=R&BillID=153

2. New HHS Data Show More Americans than Ever Have Health Coverage through the Affordable Care Act. (Press release) June 5, 2021. **https://www.cms.gov/newsroom/press-releases/new-hhs-data-show-more-americans-ever-have-health-coverage-through-affordable-care-act**

3. Kinship Care and the Child Welfare System. May 5, 2022. Children's Bureau/ACYF/ACF/HHS. https://www.childwelfare.gov

NOTES

NOTES

www.ingramcontent.com/pod-product-compliance
Lightning Source LLC
Chambersburg PA
CBHW081156020426
42333CB00020B/2526